JOHN BROWN
OF
HARPER'S FERRY

WITH CONTEMPORARY PRINTS, PHOTOGRAPHS, AND MAPS

JOHN ANTHONY SCOTT
ROBERT ALAN SCOTT

Facts On File
New York

John Brown of Harper's Ferry

Facts On File, Inc.
460 Park Avenue South
New York NY 10016
USA

Library of Congress Cataloging-in-Publication Data

Scott, John Anthony, 1916-
    John Brown of Harper's Ferry

    (Makers of America)
    Bibliography: p.
    Includes index.
    Summary: Describes the life of the abolitionist whose struggle to free American slaves resulted in the raid on Harper's Ferry.
    1. Brown, John, 1800–1859. 2. Abolitionists—United States—Biography. 3. Harper's Ferry (W. Va.)—History—John Brown's Raid, 1859. 4. Slavery—United States—Anti-slavery movements. [1. Brown, John, 1800–1859. 2. Abolitionists. 3. Harper's Ferry (W. Va.)—History—John Brown's Raid, 1859. 4. Slavery—Anti-slavery movements] I. Scott, Robert Alan. II. Title. III. Series.
E176.M23 [E451]   973.6'6'0924 [B] [92] 87-9071
ISBN 0-8160-1347-0

A British CIP catalogue record for this book is available from the British Library.

Facts On File books are available at special discounts when purchased in bulk quantities for businesses, associations, institutions or sales promotions. Please call our Special Sales Department in New York at 212/683-2244 (dial 800/322-8755 except in NY, AK or HI).

Text design by Debbie Glasserman
Jacket design by Duane Stapp
Composition by Facts On File Inc.
Manufactured by Haddon Craftsmen, Inc.
Printed in the United States of America

10 9 8 7 6 5 4 3

This book is printed on acid-free paper.

In memory of
LOUIS RUCHAMES
devoted John Brown student, colleague and friend

ACKNOWLEDGMENTS

The authors acknowledge with gratitude the use of facilities and resources made available by the following centers: Amherst College Library, Boston Public Library, Columbia University Library, Fieldston School Library, Kansas State Historical Society, the Library of Congress, Massachusetts Historical Society, the National Archives, Ohio Historical Society, Old Sturbridge Village Library, Portsmouth (Virginia) Public Library, West Virginia Department of Culture and History. We found the symposium "John Brown and the Springfield Community," presented by the Connecticut Valley Historical Museum, February 21, 1987, to be of great value.

Paul D. Escott of the University of North Carolina at Charlotte, and Douglas T. Miller of Michigan State University read the manuscript and offered suggestions and corrections for which we are very grateful. Many thanks to Emmy Hastings, who drew the maps which appear in this book, for her excellent work. Jamie Warren and Claire Johnston of Facts On File provided, always cheerfully, invaluable editorial support.

CONTENTS

PROLOGUE

Some of Virginia's soldiers could not help admiring the old man they had come to hang. Arms roped to his sides at the elbows, he climbed the scaffold willingly and shook hands with his executioners. As they got him ready, they offered one last favor: should they drop a handkerchief to give the final order for the hanging, one of them asked, so he would not hear it? The condemned man's voice "sounded to me unnaturally natural—so composed was its tone," an officer who was nearby recalled. "He replied that it did not matter to him, if only they would not keep him too long waiting."

But the 1,500 soldiers, many of them young and green, took ten minutes to find their places in formation around the prisoner. He stood there, feet lashed together, quiet and still. It was a pleasant day, that December 2, 1859, in Charles Town, Virginia. A warm breeze from the south played with the linen that covered John Brown's face.

John Wilkes Booth, who accompanied the First Virginia Regiment from Richmond, looked on him with the contempt a traitor deserves. Thomas J. Jackson—a brilliant general who was later known as "Stonewall" Jackson—saw a brave but misguided man on the scaffold and sent a "fervent petition" to heaven for his soul, which he feared "might receive the sentence, 'Depart, ye wicked, into everlasting fire.'"

For, however noble his intentions, Brown had done great wrong. Even people who shared his goals would not deny it. He, who viewed slavery as a brutal war against a helpless people, had butchered unarmed men in the name of freedom—men who didn't even own slaves. He proclaimed "the great family of man" but would listen to no one, not even young men who put their lives in his hands. And so, though he was a skilled guerrilla fighter and a bold strategist, he botched in a single day the great liberation campaign he'd been planning for decades. All he did in the end was kill people in a sleepy mountain town, lead his men to death, and leave his family destitute.

"We are ready," someone called out. Now the trap fell and he was gone. "So perish all such enemies of Virginia, all such enemies of the Union, all such foes of the human race!" an officer declared as the body swung.

They left him there more than half an hour. Then they took John Brown's body down and let his widow haul it home for burial in the frozen earth of the Adirondack mountains.

What he had done was unthinkable to most people at the time. But before long many tens of thousands were doing the same. Soon the men who hanged him as a traitor were traitors themselves; killing, dying and leaving families to grieve in a land laid waste by war—all for the sake of the right to own human property. Many thousands followed Brown out of the North to fight, liberate slaves, and arm them against the slaveholders. They revered him as a patriot, prophet, and martyr.

He was a loner who died at the crest of a rising tide. His personal tragedy was the focus of a nation's torment. His dream became a nation's cause.

This is his story.

1

BLOW YE THE TRUMPET
Harper's Ferry, 1859

> Blow ye the trumpet in Zion, and sound an alarm in my holy mountain; let all the inhabitants tremble, for the judgement of the Lord is at hand.
> —The Book of Joel

The evening of Sunday, October 16, 1859, was dark and rainy in Maryland's Blue Ridge mountains. A group of men filed quietly away from a small farmhouse down a dirt road toward Harper's Ferry, a little more than five miles to the south. They carried rifles on their shoulders, and pistols were buckled at their belts. All went on foot except the leader, John Brown, who drove an old wagon with a single horse between the shafts. Brown was fifty-nine years of age. "He stooped somewhat," a friend remembered, "and was rather narrow-shouldered—went looking on the ground almost all the time, with his head bent forward, apparently in study or in thought."

John Brown was an old man; his companions were young. Most of them were still in their twenties. Three, Owen, Watson, and Oliver, were John Brown's sons; two, William and Dauphin Thompson, were neighbors from North Elba, in New York's Adirondack mountains, where the Browns had their home. Seventeen of the group were white and five—Osborne Anderson, John Anthony Copeland, Shields

Green, Lewis Leary, and Dangerfield Newby—were black. Nineteen in all went down the Harper's Ferry road that night; Owen Brown and two others stayed behind at the farmhouse to bring down a heavy load of weapons and supplies to a schoolhouse not far from Harper's Ferry and near the Potomac River.

By ten o'clock that night Brown's men reached a wooded hill called Maryland Heights, which marked one side of a huge cleft in the wall of the Blue Ridge mountains. Here the Potomac and the Shenandoah rivers came together and flowed eastward through the gap. Thomas Jefferson visited this spot three quarters of a century before Brown's men came there. "The passage of the Potomac through the Blue Ridge," wrote Jefferson, "is perhaps one of the most stupendous scenes in nature." As he watched the river flowing through the mountain wall at the foot of mighty crags, Jefferson had the feeling that long ago the waters had been dammed up in the hills; they went on rising until at last they "broke over at this spot and tore the mountain down from its summit to its base." Maryland Heights, two thousand feet above sea level, marked the water gap on the northern side; Loudoun Heights marked it on the south.

The narrow V-shaped strip of rocky land where the Potomac and the Shenandoah came together was called Harper's Ferry. (See Map 1.) There during the late 1790's the federal government began to build an armory, or a place both to manufacture guns and to stockpile them. George Washington, who was at that time president of the United States, himself chose the site. Washington understood very well how easily the waterpower of the two rivers could be harnessed to run the machines in the federal factories. He was determined, too, that the national government should forge its own weapons, and not have to buy them at the fancy prices that private businessmen were charging.

By the end of the War of 1812 Harper's Ferry was a quiet little factory town with mills and machine shops and workers' homes huddled together on that rocky neck of land between the rivers and in the suburb of Bolivar Heights directly to the

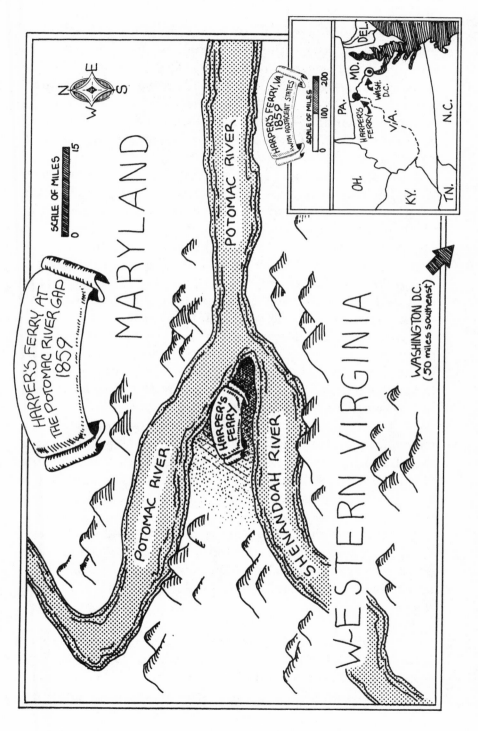

west. By 1858, the year before John Brown came, a skilled work force of four hundred machinists and armorers was producing and assembling thousands of muskets and rifles every year; the town's population had risen to well over three thousand.

John Brown and his men had three objectives there: the musket factory, the rifle works and the arsenal where many of the weapons produced at Harper's Ferry were stored.

The largest and most important of these was the musket factory. Muskets were the standard weapon of the time. Their barrels were smooth and loaded with powder and ball at the muzzle. The factory had machine shops, warehouses, and offices housed in about twenty buildings which hugged a narrow strip of land between the hills and the Potomac River. A high brick wall enclosed the compound, with its gate at the east end, near the center of town. (For the location of the musket factory, the rifle works and the arsenal, see Map 2.)

A half mile away down the Shenandoah River a newer type of weapon was produced at the rifle works on Lower Hall Island. These guns had "rifled" or grooved barrels so that the bullets fired from them flew with a spin. Because rifles could hit targets with much greater accuracy than muskets, they were the favored weapon of hunters, frontiersmen, and sharpshooters. John Hall, an inventor from Maine, designed the rifles produced at Harper's Ferry. Hall's rifles were loaded at the breech, not, like almost all the firearms of that day, at the muzzle. A lot of army people thought of the Hall rifle as the weapon of the future.

Some of the finished weapons manufactured at Harper's Ferry were sent out to be stored in federal arsenals in other parts of the country. But some of these weapons were stockpiled in the federal arsenal at Harper's Ferry itself. This arsenal consisted of two buildings that lay almost directly opposite the musket factory gate.

Two railroads linked Harper's Ferry with the outside world: the Baltimore and Ohio, and the Winchester and Potomac. All railroad trains as well as horsedrawn carts and coaches crossed back and forth between Harper's Ferry and

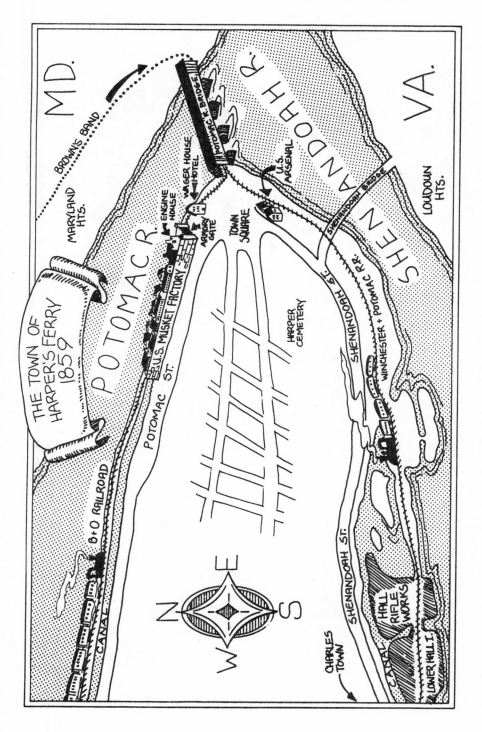

The United States Armory at Harper's Ferry (about 1856)

This is a view of Harper's Ferry, looking toward the southeast. On the left the Potomac River is flowing toward the bridge that spans it. Beyond the bridge the river joins with the Shenandoah, then flows out of the picture in the distance on the left hand side. On the extreme left is the Maryland shore, rising up to Maryland Heights. The Harper's Ferry armory lies along the Potomac River shore on its right hand side. The numerous workshops, storehouses and other government buildings that compose the armory are clearly shown. Looking closely one may see a train puffing along the Baltimore and Ohio Railroad tracks toward Wheeling (now West) Virginia. On the right hand side of the picture Harper's Ferry itself rises up to a rocky height. Beyond, Loudoun Heights rise up in their majesty.
—Beyes Album of Virginia, *1857*

Maryland at the Potomac River toll bridge. *(To follow the struggle in Harper's Ferry, refer from here on to the large-scale Map 3.)* This was a covered bridge, built rather like a great long barn, with a wooden roof to protect the timbers from rain and the danger of rot.

Brown's raiders came down to this Potomac River bridge from Maryland Heights at ten o'clock that Sunday night. They crossed the bridge, seized the night watchman, and put out their own guards. Then they moved on to the musket factory gate a couple of hundred yards away, made a prisoner of the guard, and broke into the compound. "They told me,"

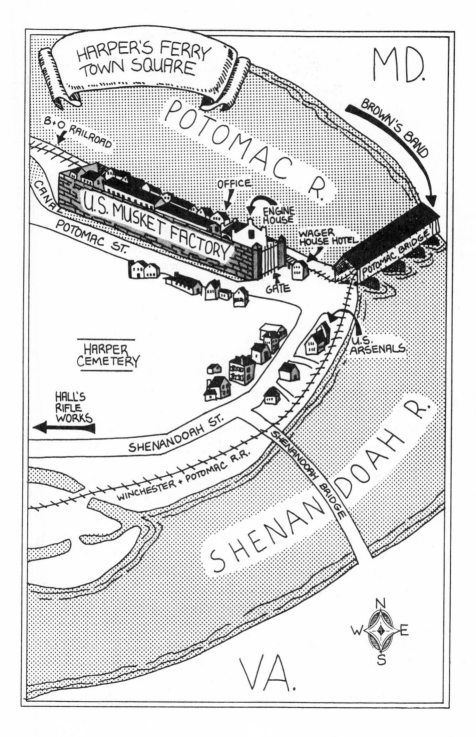

the man remembered later, "to make no noise, or else they would put me into eternity."

These two guards—the man at the Potomac River bridge and the one at the musket factory gate—were the first of many prisoners that the raiders took that night and the following Monday morning; workers in the factories, lock tenders from the canals, armory officials, planters and their slaves, townsfolk. Brown's men herded these people into the enginehouse, which lay directly to the left of the musket factory gate. This enginehouse, divided by a partition into two spaces, contained firefighting apparatus; today we would call it a fire station. All in all, the raiders took well over sixty prisoners, though, to be sure, many escaped. There, at the enginehouse, they would remain in one or other of its rooms until the raid was over, huddled together shivering in the damp and cold, hungry and thirsty, menaced by the terror and death and bloodshed that surrounded them, the bullets zinging overhead and sometimes smacking with thud and shatter into doors and windows and human beings. Most eminent of these prisoners was Colonel Lewis Washington, Jefferson County planter and a great-grandnephew of George Washington himself. The humblest of the prisoners was John Malloy, a retarded youth who slept in doorways and fetched water for the townspeople from the town pump or the river in return for scraps of bread and meat from their tables.

With the musket factory in his hands, John Brown sent men out to occupy the arsenal. Others seized the Shenandoah River bridge and the rifle works on Lower Hall Island. Yet another group of raiders moved westward into Jefferson county to capture planters and to bring the news of the uprising to their slaves.

So far everything had gone smoothly for John Brown. But in the very first minutes of the new day, Monday, October 17, trouble came. The first person to sound the alarm was the relief watchman on the Potomac River bridge, who walked up to the bridge to take over his post shortly after midnight. Challenged by Brown's guards he fled back along the tracks of the Baltimore and Ohio Railroad to the Wager House

Hotel, a restaurant and an inn directly opposite the station platform. "Armed men on the bridge!" he cried.

The baggage attendant at the station, a black man named Hayward Shepherd, was not as lucky as the watchman. A little later he walked up to the bridge to see what was going on, and was challenged. Brown's guards shot him in the back; he collapsed in front of the station in agony. Dragged inside, he died some hours later.

A little after one o'clock that Monday morning, a clerk from the Wager House Hotel flagged down the night express as it came toward Harper's Ferry along the Baltimore and Ohio tracks from the west. "Armed men on the bridge!" Panic-stricken passengers milled around on the train, spilled out onto the platform, took refuge in the hotel. John Brown talked with the train's conductor, and gave permission for it to pass on its way. After some delay, the train rumbled over the Potomac River bridge into Maryland, headed toward Baltimore. Soon, just as John Brown hoped, the alarm was speeding over the telegraph wires and making headlines in the nation's papers:

FEARFUL AND EXCITING INTELLIGENCE! NEGRO INSURRECTION AT HARPER'S FERRY!! HARPER'S FERRY BRIDGE FORTIFIED BY ARMED MEN AND DEFENDED WITH CANNON!!! ARMS SEIZED AND SENT INTO THE INTERIOR!!!!!

The railroad conductor wired that there were one hundred and fifty raiders. At first there was disbelief; then panic spread. Slave revolts had always been the deepest dread of plantation owners. Here was an insurrection led by whites and coming when the country was already in turmoil over slavery.

This news awaited John B. Floyd, United States secretary for war, when he arrived in his Washington, D.C., office later that morning. John B. Floyd was a Virginia lawyer who, like his father before him, had served a term as governor of the state of Virginia. In 1861, little more than a year after John

Brown's raid, he would be commissioned as a general in the Confederate army. He was surprised by the news, but it shouldn't really have surprised him. In August 1859, just a couple of months before the raid happened, he had received an unsigned letter. John Brown and his private army were in Maryland, the letter said; they planned to attack a federal arsenal there in just a few weeks. John B. Floyd wasn't excited; it must, he thought, be idle gossip or rumor. There was, after all, no federal arsenal in Maryland. So he filed the letter in the crank file, and forgot about it. Now, when he walked into the War Office, here was this telegram: *Armed men at Harper's Ferry!*

The secretary for war moved into action. He talked with the president of the United States, and sent out an order for artillery and marines to move up to the Ferry. Then he called in his friend Colonel Robert E. Lee to see him. Colonel Lee was the master of Arlington, an estate with a fine mansion house just across the Potomac from Washington, D.C. Lee, a professional cavalry officer, came from an old Virginia family, just like Floyd himself, and had at one time served as the superintendent of West Point. Floyd asked Lee to take charge of the federal forces that were being sent into battle against John Brown. Along with Lee as his aide, Floyd sent Lieutenant J.E.B. Stuart, a young cavalry officer.

The marines were stationed at the Washington Navy Yard. It took time for them to get out their guns and ammunition, to put on their best uniforms (dark blue topcoats and sky-blue pants), and to make the trip by train to Harper's Ferry. Lee and his men did not reach the armory gate until 11:00 p.m. on Monday night.

At Harper's Ferry the people moved against John Brown with a speed that took him quite by surprise. At dawn on Monday morning the pastor of the Lutheran Church on Bolivar Heights was ringing the church bell to warn the people of invasion. Soon the bells were ringing at Charles Town, the county seat of Jefferson County, in which Harper's Ferry was located. Rumor spread fast, puffing up like a balloon as it was borne upon the wind, and spreading panic.

Some said that a band of armed robbers had descended upon the town, looting and burning the houses and shooting the inhabitants. Others said no; it was a strike of canal workers demonstrating for higher wages and rampaging in a riot. Dogs barked; barefoot children scurried up and down; sleepy militiamen pulled on their boots, picked up their muskets or rifles, and straggled out onto the Charles Town green. Well before midday, as rain clouds loomed overhead, two companies of these militiamen boarded a train and were rushed at breakneck speed—thirty-five miles per hour, no less—along the tracks of the Winchester and Potomac Railroad in the direction of Harper's Ferry.

Militiamen were simply ordinary civilians, the men who lived in America's towns and villages. Ever since colonial days they had been trained to muster on the greens whenever the church bells tolled and brought news of an emergency, like an attack by Native Americans.

Outside Harper's Ferry, Colonel John T. Gibson, commanding, unloaded his men and moved them in on foot. Gibson sent one company around Harper's Ferry to the north, with instructions to cross the Potomac by boat about a mile upstream. This company, once across the river, followed the route that the raiders had taken the night before, came back into Harper's Ferry across the Potomac River bridge, and drove Brown's guards away. Gibson's other company moved directly into Harper's Ferry from the west—over Bolivar Heights and down the Shenandoah Road to the center of town.

This counterattack by the Charles Town militiamen developed between the hours of twelve and one on Monday afternoon. Up to this time only townspeople had been killed or mortally wounded, for instance, Hayward Shepherd, the black baggage handler. Now Brown's men began to fall.

The first of these was Dangerfield Newby, one of the three raiders assigned to guard the Shenandoah River bridge. Newby was a Virginian. The son of a Scottish father and a black slave woman, he was born in Fauquier County. When his father freed him he went to live in Ohio, leaving his wife

Charles Town militiamen rally to the defense of Harper's Ferry

The militia includes men of all ages, from beardless boys to grizzled veterans. Only a few are fortunate enough to have mounts for the trek from Charles Town to the Ferry. They carry a variety of weapons: pistols, muskets, a bayonet, knives, or swords. One dignified gentleman with a high hat, by the horse's head, walks along armed with nothing more dangerous than a walking stick. Stragglers bring up the rear.
—Harper's Weekly Magazine, *November 26, 1859*

Harriet and their seven children in bondage. Dangerfield's painful struggle to earn money so that he might buy his family's freedom proved fruitless; this was why he joined John Brown. Force alone, he thought, could overthrow slavery and liberate Harriet and the children. In the long hours of waiting at the Kennedy farm before the raid began, Dangerfield read Harriet's letters over and over again. "Come this fall without fail," she had written, "I want to see you so much! This is the bright hope that I have before me."

When the militiamen attacked the Shenandoah bridge, Newby, along with Oliver Brown and William Thompson was forced to flee. Oliver and William made it across the town square to the safety of the armory gate; Newby was hit by a militiaman's slug. He fell on the cobblestones with a huge gash in his throat and lay still in a red and spreading pool.

The townspeople, encouraged by the arrival of the militia, joined in the attack. At about one o'clock a detachment of citizens stormed the rifle works on Lower Hall Island. Brown's little garrison there consisted of John Henry Kagi, John Anthony Copeland and Lewis Sheridan Leary. Kagi, a young schoolteacher from Ohio, was second in command of Brown's forces. He was an intelligent, outspoken person who hated slavery from the bottom of his heart and who thought of freedom for all Americans, black as well as white, as "a future reward for mankind." His comrades, John Anthony Copeland and Lewis Sheridan Leary, were free men of color born in North Carolina; both had moved to Oberlin, Ohio. Leary, like his father before him, was a saddle and harness maker; he left a wife and child behind him in Oberlin when he joined John Brown.

As the morning hours passed, Kagi waited at the rifle works with mounting rage and frustration for a message from John Brown. Brown's plan, as he knew, was to gather his forces at the Ferry; meet up with Owen Brown and his helpers, who were to bring the arms and other supplies by wagon down from the schoolhouse; and then move out across the Shenandoah bridge to Loudoun Heights on the south. What on earth, Kagi thought, was the old man waiting for? Very soon it would be too late to move across the Shenandoah, or to retreat in any other direction. They would all be caught on that rocky point between the two rivers like rats in a trap.

But the order to move out never came; by early afternoon Kagi and his two companions were surrounded by their attackers on the three land sides of Hall Island. They leaped from a window in the rifle works into the Shenandoah, and began to swim. Kagi was hit: his body floated downstream. Leary, like Kagi, was hit while swimming and mortally wounded. The townsfolk brought him ashore and left him to die alone in a work shed on Lower Hall Island. As for Copeland, he was captured unharmed.

Throughout the morning John Brown was waiting for the slaves, and maybe freemen, too, whom he hoped would join him when the word got around that he had taken Harper's

Ferry. Only a handful showed up. He planned to arm his recruits with guns and pikes brought down from the Kennedy farm to the little schoolhouse by the Potomac; at dawn he had sent two of his men back across the river with a large captured wagon. They had orders to join Owen Brown and his team in transporting weapons and supplies, first to the schoolhouse, and then across the Potomac River bridge into Harper's Ferry. They were soon cut off by militiamen and could not return. Raiders, guns, ammunition, and camp supplies, all remained on the Maryland side of the river.

John Brown waited too long. By two o'clock in the afternoon his position was hopeless and escape impossible. Armed men swarmed all over town—on Bolivar Heights, at the bridges, on the streets, and along the riverbanks. Brown, with a handful of raiders and a crowd of hostages, was trapped in the enginehouse near the armory gate. There was nothing left for him to do but to ask for a truce, so that he might talk with the soldiers and arrange conditions under which he and the surviving raiders would be allowed to leave town. Perhaps, he thought, they would be allowed to escape if they agreed to free the prisoners once well outside Harper's Ferry.

Early in the afternoon Brown sent William Thompson out with a white flag, with instructions to make his way over to the Wager House Hotel, where the military had set up their headquarters. But those who had seen their town attacked and their neighbors killed were in no mood for talking. Grabbing Thompson, they carried him off to the hotel and locked him up. Brown tried again. This time he sent out his own son, Watson.

At twenty-four, Watson was in the prime of life, a magnificent-looking man over six feet tall with dark hair and clear brown eyes. John and Mary Brown had raised him to believe that to abolish slavery was a duty a young American owed his country and humanity. Watson was a hardworking farmer and shepherd, and his father's loyal son. He left behind him a young wife and a baby boy when he followed John Brown to Harper's Ferry. "Oh, Bell," he had written shortly before the raid, "I want to see you and the little fellow very much. . . . I sometimes think that we shall not meet again."

As soon as Watson appeared at the armory gate, a shot felled him. He crawled back to the enginehouse and lay twisting in pain.

John Brown tried once more. This time he sent out Aaron Stevens, "a remarkably fine-looking young man," an eyewitness said, "his hair was black and his eyes of dark hazel had a very penetrating glance. . . ." Stevens, too, was shot, and fell bleeding to the ground. Now Joseph Brewer, one of the hostages, strode out into the street. He picked up Stevens, carried him over to the Wager House Hotel, then returned to the armory and took his place again among the shivering prisoners.

In the horror of these moments Willie Leeman was seized with panic. Twenty years old and one of the youngest of the raiders, Leeman was described as "only a boy, who smoked a great deal and drank a little, . . . very handsome and very attractive." He dashed across the armory compound, leaped over the railroad line and jumped down into the Potomac below. A couple of townsfolk or militiamen rowed out to the youngster and shot him in the head. A reporter at the scene the next day wrote that "his black hair may just be seen floating on the surface of the water, waving with every ripple."

Soon after this, one of the raiders in the enginehouse took aim at a man out in the street, and, heedless of the anguished cries of protest from the prisoners, killed him. The victim was Fountain Beckham, mayor of Harper's Ferry and a person well loved in the community. Now the fury of the townspeople rose to new heights. A mob rushed over to the Wager House Hotel, broke into the room where William Thompson was being held, and prepared to kill him. Christina Fouke, sister of the hotel proprietor, placed herself between Thompson and his assassins. "Leave him alone!" she cried.

They brushed her aside and dragged him by the throat into the street. Thompson, who was 26, had left a wife in North Elba to go with his brother Dauphin and John Brown. The two families were closely linked. Brown's daughter, Ruth, had married another of the Thompson brothers, Henry. One of his sons, Watson Brown, had married William's sister.

Now he screamed at the men as they dragged him to the Potomac River bridge. "Eighty thousand will arise up to avenge me and carry out my purpose of giving liberty to the slaves."

At the bridge, two men fired into his head and, one of them later testified, "before he fell a dozen more balls were buried in him." They threw his body into the river and left it face up in the shallow water.

Daylight was fading; militiamen from neighboring towns continued to pour into Harper's Ferry. Across the Shenandoah to the south a flock of crows circled Loudoun Heights; the air was loud with the beating of wings.

John E. Cook, one of the raiders who was left on the other side of the Potomac, climbed Maryland Heights and saw the militia and townspeople pouring their fire into the engine-house. He shot at them from a tree and they shot back, severing a small limb he had ahold of and sending him crashing to the ground. Cook made his way back to the schoolhouse and reported to Owen and the other raiders there. They hid in the woods for the night, then climbed into the mountains and headed north.

Harper's Ferry hotels and saloons filled up with drinking men; the darkening streets resounded with screams, curses, and the bang of guns. The raiders who had set out from the Kennedy farm nearly twenty-four hours earlier were almost all scattered and gone. Some were fleeing, some were captive, some dead, and some dying.

John Brown had barricaded himself in the enginehouse; there he waited quietly for what the morning would bring. A small group of hostages shared the vigil with him. Four raiders stood beside him—Edwin Coppoc, Dauphin Thompson, Jeremiah Anderson, and Shields Green. Watson and his younger brother, Oliver, lay on the floor, dying.

All the men shivered in the bitter cold, none had tasted a morsel of food since the early morning. Brown himself had not eaten since the night before. He paced back and forth, red-eyed from fatigue, his face begrimed with gunsmoke.

Late that Monday evening Colonel Lee arrived, and posted his marines at the armory to stand guard. Then he sat down and wrote a letter to John Brown. "It is impossible for you to escape," wrote Lee, "the Armory is surrounded on all sides by troops . . . Colonel Lee, United States Army, . . . sent by the President of the United States to suppress the insurrection . . . demands the surrender of the persons in the Armory buildings."

Tuesday morning, October 18, 1859, at 7 a.m., Lieutenant Stuart passed Lee's letter to Brown through a crack in the enginehouse door. The two men talked briefly. Surrender, Stuart told Brown, must be unconditional; there would be no discussion of terms. After a few moments of conversation, Stuart moved away from the door and waved his hat. Using a ladder as a battering ram the marines moved in to the attack.

John Brown's Last Stand in the Firehouse

The artist has sketched the scene in the firehouse as he has imagined it just before Colonel Lee and the marines made the assault in the early morning of October 18, 1859. In the middle of the building stands the firefighter's wagon and pump, and to the right of it the canvas hose wound up on a huge wagon wheel spool. John Brown stands silhouetted against the gate upon the left. Behind him some of his hostages stand waiting quietly for whatever the morning will bring. In the foreground Oliver lies upon the ground, almost dead. Watson is slumped against the wagon, dying. Shields Green is seen against the right-hand door, armed with a pike. The artist shows Brown's men as a group of nine. In actuality they were only seven.

—Frank Leslie's Illustrated News, *November 5, 1859*

In three minutes it was all over. Two raiders, Dauphin Thompson and Jeremiah Anderson, lay dead; one marine was dying. Edwin Coppoc and Shields Green were taken prisoner. Brown himself was stretched on the floor bleeding from sword cuts on his head and shoulders. He, along with Aaron Stevens, was carried away to the paymaster's office next door to the enginehouse, and covered with blankets.

People crowded around John Brown—journalists, soldiers, townsfolk; soon all sorts of important people were arriving, senators, congressmen and the like, and among them Governor Henry Wise of Virginia. The governor looked curiously at the old man as he lay there on the floor, his hair and beard matted with blood, "a broken-winged hawk, with a fearless eye, and his talons set for further fight, if need be."

The crowd began to fire questions at the wounded leader.

"What was your object in coming?" asked one.

"We came to free the slaves, and only that," Brown replied.

"Upon what principles do you justify your acts?" said another.

"I pity the poor in bondage, that have none to help them," Brown answered. "That is why I am here, not to gratify any personal animosity, revenge or vindictive spirit. It is my sympathy with the wronged and the oppressed, that are as good as you, and as precious in the sight of God."

"Did you expect to hold Harper's Ferry for any considerable time?" asked a congressman from Ohio.

"I do not know whether I ought to reveal my plans," Brown answered, "this question is still to be settled, this Negro question, I mean. The end of that is not yet."

2

SOWING THE DRAGON'S TEETH
African-American Slavery in the United States

> Cadmus, founder of Thebes, killed a dragon and scattered its teeth over the earth. These seeds sprang up as armed men who fell upon each other and spilled blood.

Harper's Ferry was a prelude to the Civil War that broke out in 1861 and that engulfed the country in four long years of bloodletting. It was a mutter of thunder foretelling the boom of cannon, when not just a handful of Americans, but tens of thousands, would come to blows in a savage reckoning over the existence of slavery in the American Union. People have asked, what led John Brown and the American nation to the shedding of blood? What was the soil upon which the seeds of this conflict were sown, and from which it sprang?

Harper's Ferry had its roots in two centuries of African-American enslavement. It all began in quite a small way in the early 17th century. The English settlers were establishing themselves up and down the coast from Massachusetts to Virginia; they were shorthanded in all the work that they had to do. They had, for starters, to girdle trees, clear fields, sow seed, move rocks and pile them into walls, tend cattle and sheep, set up saw mills, raise houses and barns, build ships. The only available sources of power were manpower and animal power, aided fitfully by the power of water and wind. There were no steam engines, no electricity or electric turbines, no gasoline tractors or saws, no earth movers or mechanical cranes.

Much of what had to be done a man and woman might accomplish together, with the help of their family; and this in fact was the fate of most settlers—to do hard work for long hours and to remain quite poor. But men who were ambitious to get rich, and who had a little money to invest at the start, needed much more help; they needed lots of servants. William Penn, the English Quaker who founded the colony of Pennsylvania in 1680, put it well. In a tract written in 1684 to promote his colony, he pointed out that there were many poor people in Europe who wanted to emigrate but who could not afford the passage. Bring in as many of these people as you

The Storming of the Firehouse

This is the scene at the moment when Colonel Lee and his men take the firehouse by assault, seen from the outside. The storming party has just battered the door down with a ladder and is moving in to the attack. One marine, mortally wounded, lies in the foreground.
—Harper's Weekly Magazine, *November 26, 1859*

can, he advised his readers, because their labor would be the key to wealth in the New World. "The poor," he wrote, "are the hands and feet of the rich. It is their labor that improves countries; and to encourage them is to promote the real benefit of the public."

People were indeed anxious to leave Europe and to try their fortunes in the New World; many poor white servants came over to America during the 17th and 18th centuries. Some of them, to be sure, were kidnapped or brought over by force—like children from the streets of London or soldiers taken in battle and made prisoners of war. But most of the servants came of their own free will, driven by hunger and by the hope that they would find something better than they had known before.

There were never enough of these white servants to meet the demand of wealthier settlers for labor. These whites were free men and women who bound themselves to work for a term of years in order to cover the cost of their ocean trip. They did a few years of backbreaking labor and then, if they survived the ordeal, their service ended. *Temporary* servants or bondspeople were always turning into *totally* free workers—free to quit service, to settle elsewhere, to begin an independent life of their own. On the whole, for these poor white folk, the wheel of fortune turned only in one direction, from servitude to freedom.

Farmers and planters, who were the biggest employers of labor in the colonies, therefore, began to supplement the European labor supply with workers from another source. By the 17th century the slave trade was bringing in huge numbers of Africans to the Caribbean islands. The Portuguese began this trade in the 15th century, and in the 16th century the Spanish followed in their footsteps; the English, the Dutch, and the French took the same path soon after. Well before the end of the 17th century, Boston, New York, and Rhode Island sea captains, attracted like buzzards by the profits to be reaped, entered the trade. The basis was laid for an enormous expansion of the number of African-American servants imported to the North American coast.

Most of the Africans brought in to North America were sold to Southern planters for use in Virginia, Maryland, and South Carolina; but Northern colonists took their share of slaves too. Slaves planted and harvested tobacco in Virginia and Maryland, rice in South Carolina, wheat in eastern Pennsylvania and the Hudson Valley. They raised fine horses on the Narragansett Plantations of Rhode Island. They served in the houses of the rich as coachmen, stablemen, footmen, dairy and garden workers, maidservants and musicians. They plied their trades as carpenters, harpooners, dockworkers, ploughmen, and more. They helped small farmers to cultivate their crops both North and South, and worked beside them in the fields. African-American slaves in uncounted numbers, along with many thousands of white servants, laid the foundations of the new society.

As the white servants became free some of them rose in the social scale, but the black people, in sharp contrast, were forced downwards into lifelong servitude. Whites began to view African-Americans as a class apart to be hated, feared, and despised. Slavery set its own unique and tragic stamp upon the African immigrants to this country. No other immigrant group was branded in this way.

In the first place the law in each colony set the African-Americans apart. The law said that these people were property, like cattle, horses, or household goods. White people were entitled to buy and sell them, to give them away as gifts, to put them up as prizes in a raffle, to pass them on to their children by the provisions of their wills. Owners were entitled to use slaves in the same way as they used animals; they could make them work for as long and hard as they pleased, without pay. They could punish them for real or imaginary faults as harshly as they wished; they could use terror to keep defiant slaves in line. Slaves who fired their owners' barns, who ran away, who struck back when they were struck, were hunted like beasts, tortured, branded, hung in chains, even burnt alive at the stake.

African-Americans, in the second place, were set apart and kept under control not by man-made brands like the ones used to brand cattle, but by a brand that nature itself had set upon them. The single most important brand, or badge, of American slavery, was the color of the skin. Not all people with dark skins, to be sure, were slaves in colonial society; a tiny minority of black people were free. This made little difference. By the end of the 17th century whites thought of all people with dark skin as slaves, and treated them accordingly. To have a dark skin—to be black, coffee-colored, or red-skinned—meant to whites, quite simply, that one was a person who either had very few rights or none. Blacks, whether free or slave, had *no birthright.* If a slave's father was a free man, that hardly helped him at all. If his mother was a slave, he inherited nothing from her, except the condition of being a slave for life. African-Americans, whether slave or free, were not considered to be British citizens, and had no right to vote or to participate in community affairs. They could not, for the most part, fight in the militia, marry a white person, move around from place to place as they pleased, or worship with whites in church. Setting African-Americans apart in this way was easy: They were identified by the badge of a dark skin. Thus they lived their lives in isolation from almost everybody except their master and his family, and their fellow slaves.

African-American slavery endured for well over one century in the North, and for even longer in the South. Almost all whites came to accept slavery as something natural and proper. Most whites became tainted with the arrogance of the kidnappers who had seized human beings in Africa, carried them against their will across the Atlantic, and successfully reduced them to the status of beasts of burden. This racism infected all the colonies; it spilled over into new territories when after the Revolution the country expanded westward across the Appalachian Mountains. It prevailed as much in South Carolina, where there were many slaves, as in Vermont, where there were few.

As slavery grew, as the numbers of slaves exploded from a mere handful to tens of thousands, voices began to be raised in protest. The very first such protest on British-American soil was penned by Samuel Sewall in 1700. Sewall's *The Selling of*

Joseph was the first antislavery tract to be published in New England. Sewall condemned both the slave trade upon the high seas and the holding of people in bondage upon American soil. "That which God has joined together," he said, "men do boldly rend asunder; men from their country, husbands from their wives, parents from their children. How horrible is the uncleanness, mortality, if not murder, that the ships are guilty of that bring great crowds of these miserable men, and women." Sewall went on to claim for all mankind an "equal right to liberty"; freedom, he held, was a birthright for all the earth's children. "The poorest Boys and Girls within this Province," he wrote, "have the same right to life, that the richest heirs have."

By the time of the American Revolution others were following in Sewall's footsteps and denouncing slavery—revivalist ministers like John Wesley, pamphleteers like Thomas Paine, philanthropists like the Quaker Anthony Benezet, slaveholders like Thomas Jefferson and George Mason. The Revolution marked a new era in which white colonists marched off to war to defend their freedom and to win their independence from Great Britain. Many became painfully aware of the hypocrisy of a struggle for freedom waged by a people who themselves held human beings in bondage.

At the outset of the revolutionary struggle Northerners and Southerners began to go separate ways with respect to their treatment of the slaves. Northern states, committed to providing quotas of soldiers for the Continental Army, filled these quotas with the help of slaves, to whom they promised freedom and land in return for military service. A French officer who fought with Washington at Yorktown, Ludwig von Closen, got his first view of the continental troops at White Plains on July 4, 1781. No less than one-quarter of these soldiers, he estimated, were black—"Negroes, merry, confident, and sturdy."

Southerners, by contrast, were afraid to make promises to the black people, or to arm their slaves. Slaves were more numerous in the South than in the North; the danger of armed uprisings was proportionately greater. Slaveholders, too, feared mass desertions by the slaves, and their flight to the British; but they were helpless to do anything about it. They contented themselves with uttering threats of the vengeance which they would take upon fugitives—if they caught them—and upon their families. "Should there be any among the Negroes," wrote a Virginian, "wicked enough to provoke the fury of the Americans against their defenceless fathers and mothers, their wives, their women and children, let them only consider the difficulties of effecting their escape, and what they must expect to suffer if they fall into the hands of the Americans."

When the war was over, North and South continued, with respect to slavery, to follow separate paths. In the Northern states antislavery people began to turn their attention to the emancipation of the blacks; sooner or later most of these states passed laws conferring freedom upon their slaves. When these laws were first proposed, there was bitter opposition to their passage in states like New York and New Jersey, where slaves were numerous; but this opposition weakened with the passage of time. After the beginning of the 19th century, free white workers were flocking into the country through Northern ports; labor, less and less, was in short supply.

The Northern emancipation laws did not free *all* the slaves in a given state; they provided merely that the *children* of slaves born after a certain date should become free people at the age, say, of twenty-five. Slaveholders were thus given ample time to sell their older slaves in the South where they could still get a good price for them. Bondage in the North faded away not so much because the antislavery movement was strong as because the economic need for slaves had now passed. Slavery in the North died out as children came of age and as adult slaves were sold, died, or freed by their masters' consent. By mid-century there were almost no slaves left in the North at all. Most black people still living there were now legally free.

Gradual emancipation in the North was a bitter and painful experience for the black people. Families were split up as parents were sold to the South and as children were kept behind to continue life in bondage during the long years until they came of age. If this liberation of the North's slaves was, nonetheless, an historic step, it only *began* the task of truly freeing the black people; in no sense did it complete that task. Northern blacks continued to live on without the birthright of freedom which whites enjoyed. Most Northern states, though not all, continued to withhold citizenship rights from blacks, including the right to vote at elections. Black people inherited and endured, even when they became legally free, most of the horrible burdens, or badges, of their slave past. They were forced to ride in separate railroad cars, often little better than filthy cattle boxes. Their children were made to attend separate schools. Forbidden to travel *inside* stagecoaches, they must ride atop, exposed to wind, cold, and rain. They could not occupy cabins on coastal ships or river boats, dine in the same restaurants as whites, or sleep in the same inns. White workers chased them from the jobs they held, often with violence and bloodshed. They ended up with only the most menial of occupations, like sweeping streets, carrying bricks, toting bales and rolling barrels. Herded in squalid ghettoes, they lived on with poverty and disease. Then, to add insult to injury, whites pointed at their rags as proof of how dumb they were.

Emancipation in the years following the Revolution did not improve the lot of the black people of the North. Their condition of life, if anything, became more painful and more humiliating than it had been before. "They are free," wrote Fanny Kemble, famous British actress, "from the chain, the whip, the enforced task and unpaid toil of slavery; but they are not the less under a ban. Their kinship with slaves forever bars them from a full share of the freeman's inheritance of equal rights, and equal consideration and respect. All hands are extended to thrust them out, all fingers point at their dusky skins, all tongues . . . have learned to turn the name of their race into an insult and a reproach."

As a young man John Brown's anger and compassion was first aroused by the condition and the treatment of black people in the North—by a black child beaten by his master in Ohio, by black communicants herded together at the back of a church, and, always, by the fugitives from the South fleeing through the North, *as much slaves on free soil as if they had never fled.*

While Northerners were struggling with emancipation, slavery in the South was undergoing a transformation of its own. After the Revolution tobacco and rice prices slumped upon the world market. Many slaveholders faced bankruptcy, and the future of the plantation system seemed to be in doubt. Would owners be able to find a use for the tens of thousands of slaves they owned? If not, what would become of these people?

The answers to these questions were given by the Industrial Revolution then proceeding on the other side of the Atlantic in Great Britain, France, and Belgium. Steam-powered factories were springing up in Western Europe to spin cotton thread and to weave it into clothing for people all over the world. These were big changes: They spelled the coming in the first half of the 19th century of a bottomless demand for the wondrously tough, soft, and lustrous cotton fiber.

Traditionally cotton had been grown in tropical and semitropical lands: in India, the Near East, and the Caribbean islands. But a hardy variety of the plant could also be grown in a huge belt of the southern United States stretching from Georgia to Texas. When Eli Whitney, a Connecticut inventor, produced an engine, or "gin," in 1793 that would speedily separate the cotton fiber from the seed in which it was embedded, American cotton production was fairly on its way.

Whitney's gin could be operated by hand, by horsepower, or by steam. At first cotton production grew quite slowly; then at the end of the War of 1812 it began to mount by leaps and bounds. In 1816, 250,000 bales of cotton were grown, but in 1859, the year of Harper's Ferry, 4,500,000 bales were produced. This was eighteen times as much cotton as had been grown in 1816, which was in itself a boom year.

Rising demand for cotton on the world market was good news for planters in the older slave states of Maryland, Virginia and South Carolina who had too many slaves on their hands. A rising market for cotton was also a rising market for

Fugitive Slaves Dismounting from a Wagon Transport

The end of a stage in the long trip northward from the Ohio River to the Canadian border is over. Fugitives—men, women, and children, probably in a family group—dismount from a wagon in the snow. Two antislavery women "conductors" help them.
—From a painting in the Cincinnati Art Museum

slaves; the price of able-bodied black workers began to rise sharply after 1814. Some planters therefore abandoned the older states and migrated with their black property to fresh and fertile lands in the deep South. Others sold off their extra hands to "soul drivers," professional traders whose business it was to buy slaves in places where they were surplus and to sell them elsewhere for a profit to the highest bidders. It became a common sight to see black men, women, and children winding in weary files through city streets and over forest trails, or herded like animals upon the decks of sailing ships and river steamboats.

Rising cotton production demanded not only tens of thousands of new slave workers, but new land upon which to plant both slaves and crops. From 1815 until 1860 this slave-and-cotton frontier pushed rapidly westward. Hundreds of thousands of white people took part in this movement, fired with the hope of finding new and fruitful lands upon which to build and prosper. Some of these people owned a slave or two; most of them owned none, and never would. Those who profited most from the great land rush were planters and speculators who had money enough to buy large tracts, to sell some of them off as prices rose, and to use the rest for setting up plantations of their own. Those who started with a little money and who could buy land and slaves might strike it rich with hard work and good fortune. After 1814 raising cotton on as big a scale as possible was the easiest way to wealth in the South.

The explosion of "cotton slavery" and the territory that it ruled took place within the span of a single lifetime—between the time that John Brown was born in 1800 and his death in 1859. When Brown went to Harper's Ferry the "Cotton Kingdom" stretched from the shores of the Atlantic Ocean on the east to the Rio Grande on the west, from the Ohio River on the north to the Gulf of Mexico on the south. It was, in all probability, one of the largest slave empires that the world has ever known. In numbers of acres and numbers of field workers it might be compared to Rome itself at the time of Christ.

Year after year the demands of cotton production molded the life of the slaves in a harsh, unchanging routine. In January and February men and women harnessed oxen or mules, ploughed the land and prepared it for the seed. In March and April the ploughs were drawn over the land again. Boys and girls followed, scattering seed by hand in the furrows. Then gangs went through the fields in long wearisome hours of "chopping"—scraping away the weeds that sprang up around the growing plants. No sooner done, the weeds began to grow again, and again the gangs passed along the rows, chopping. No one must move too fast, nor yet fall behind. "If one falls behind," one slave wrote, "or is a moment idle, he is whipped. . . . The lash is flying from morning until night, the whole day long."

This daily toil made money for planters, merchants, and mill owners. But the slaves received little in return for their labor—a ration of corn, bacon and salt, a patch of land on which to raise chickens and vegetables.

When John Brown went to Harper's Ferry it was one hundred and sixty years since Samuel Sewall had uttered his cry of alarm at the rise of slavery in Britain's American colonies. With the passage of time the danger had not passed, it had only grown greater.

3

AND YET YOU WILL WEEP
The Young John Brown, 1800-32

Ah! as the heart grows older,
It will come to such sights colder
By and by, nor spare a sigh,
Though worlds of wanwood
leafmeal lie;
And yet you will weep, and know
why.
—Gerard Manley Hopkins, "Spring
and Fall."

Owen and Ruth Mills Brown, John Brown's father and mother, were country people born and raised in the hills that border the Connecticut River Valley on its western side. Owen supported himself and his family by farming, by tanning leather, and making shoes for village people. In 1799, after having lived for five years in Norfolk, Connecticut, the Browns moved to Torrington. There in 1800, when the 19th century was still only a few months old, Ruth Brown gave birth to her third child, a boy. "May 9 John was born," Owen wrote later, "nothing else very uncommon."

When John Brown came into the world nearly two centuries ago the United States itself was an infant nation. Roads were few and poor; there were no railroads and few canals to carry crops to market. Farmers, therefore, could make little money with which to buy things that their families needed from the outside world. Country people for the most part had to make everything for themselves, or do without.

The work that had to be done to meet essential and elementary wants fell upon all members of the family, and it never ended: Fields must be cleared and ploughed, seed sown, crops harvested and stored. Sheep must be sheared, wool spun, and cloth woven. Oxen and horses must be cared for and eggs collected; vegetables must be raised; fruit must be gathered and preserved. Wood must be cut, split and hauled in to warm the cabin all winter long against the bitter cold. Every child was a valued addition to the family. The daily struggle for survival and the isolation of the country forged strong bonds between parents and children. Members of a family were perhaps closer to each other than they are today.

When John Brown was eight years old, his mother died. Later he described this loss as "complete and permanent;" it left a terrible scar. Owen, on the other hand, lived to be an old man, dying at the age of eighty-five only three years before his son went to Harper's Ferry. Father and son grew old together and their friendship was lifelong. John's daughter, Ruth, remembered "my father's peculiar tenderness and devotion to Owen. In cold weather he always tucked the bedclothes around grandfather, when he went to bed, and would get up in the night to ask him if he slept warm, always seemed so kind and loving to him. . . ."

John Brown modeled himself on Owen. To understand the son, the beliefs that took him to Harper's Ferry and that explain in large part what he did there, it is necessary first of all to pay attention to the father.

Owen Brown, born in 1771, was a child of four when the battle of Lexington was fought and the American Revolution began. He remembered well when his own father, Captain John Brown of the Connecticut militia, marched off in 1776 to fight the British. Owen's mother Hannah—who was, of course, John Brown's grandmother—was left with the burden of caring for the family alone. She had ten children when her husband marched away; one more baby arrived soon after.

Captain Brown died in New York of a fever only a few weeks after leaving home. Years of intense suffering followed for his family. "I very well remember," Owen wrote, "the dreadful hard winter of 1778-9. The snow began to fall in November. . . . Wood could not be drawn in with teams, and was brought on men's shoulders, they going on snow shoes until paths were made hard enough to draw the wood on hand-sleds. Milling of grain could not be had, only by going a great distance; and our family was driven to the necessity of pounding corn for food. We lost that winter all our cattle, hogs and sheep."

These were years of bitter struggle. John Brown learned about them from his father's own lips. "To sacrifice everything for freedom" was for him no snatch of rhetoric from a 4th of July speech. The Revolution was to him both a reality and a sacred cause.

In 1782, when the Revolutionary War was nearing its end, the Brown family was living in Canton, Connecticut. There Owen, a boy of eleven years, witnessed what people called "a great awakening of religion." Ministers visited the town and people flocked to hear their impassioned words. As the community "awakened" to Jesus there was a new, joyful mood. Everybody, including the Browns, began to sing. This blossoming of religion made a deep impression on Owen and he became a devout Christian for the rest of his life. From childhood Owen had been afflicted with a dreadful stammer, but when he prayed the stammer vanished. He poured out his soul to God in a voice that never faltered.

In terms of Christian faith John Brown followed in his father's footsteps, being raised, as he tells us, "from earliest childhood to fear God and keep His commandments . . . " Like Owen, too, John Brown was a firm believer "in the divine authenticity of the Bible." He believed, that is, that every word in the Bible is true; he viewed it as a central and infallible guide to life. The Bible, as his daughter Ruth put it, "was his favorite volume, and he had a perfect knowledge of it." Great portions of it, indeed, he learned completely by heart.

Owen Brown and his son were both children of the great religious awakenings that continued to sweep the country, especially the backwoods districts, until the time of the Civil War. These awakenings must be placed in the tragic context of American life in those days. Hard labor existed side by side with the ever-present menace of death. Life in the back country was not only exhausting, filled with daily toil and care, but also very uncertain; there were many ways in which men, women, and children might lose their lives suddenly, without warning. Malarial fevers and infections carried off large numbers; people were swept away and drowned by streams in flood, thrown from horses or trampled, crushed by falling trees, or killed in skirmishes with Native Americans.

Under these circumstances ministers touring the country would often find receptive audiences. They visited communities in order to "awaken" people to God's word and the need for men and women to give thought to the salvation of their immortal souls.

Nobody said it better than Jonathan Edwards, greatest of the Connecticut River valley preachers. "Oh, sinners!" he said at Enfield, Connecticut, in 1741. "Consider the fearful danger you are in! You hang by a slender thread, with the flames of divine wrath flashing about it . . . and you have nothing to lay hold of to save yourself, nothing to keep off the flames of wrath, nothing that you have ever done, nothing that you can ever do to induce God to spare you for one moment."

As the awful meaning of the message sank in, cries and groans would rise from the throng. A frenzy of shock and fear would sweep the crowd, but with it a thrill of awakening to the reality of eternity and the holy work of preparing to meet God. Awakened communities would organize themselves and raise funds for meeting houses, ministers, and Christian education for the children.

Owen Brown, and his son John after him, were both "awakened" people. They believed that while men and women were beset daily by toil and care, they must not lose sight of their eternal souls; they must prepare to meet God free of the taint of sin; they must perform their duty not only to their families but to all people.

Owen and John Brown both considered that slavery was the supreme evil of the American world. "I am an abolitionist," Owen wrote in the 1850s ". . . I know we are not loved by many." "Abolitionist," as Owen used the term, meant far more than the belief that slavery was wrong and ought to be abolished. It was the belief, too, that all people, regardless of skin color, were equal under God and should have equal rights in America. Owen and John Brown were certain that God made *no* distinction based on color. In this belief they were proud members of an unpopular minority; both were unusual people in the racist climate of the 19th-century American world.

Owen's abolitionist beliefs were firmly rooted in the hard years of his childhood. In 1776 Captain John Brown marched off to war, as Owen later wrote his children, "and left his work undone." In August of that year one of Hannah Brown's neighbors "let my mother have the labor of his slave to plough for a few days. I used to go into the field with this slave—called Sam—and he used to carry me on his back, and I fell in love with him." Alas for Owen, the slave whose name was Sam fell sick and died. Owen cried over the grave. He had lost a friend and a second father.

Growing up a devout Christian, Owen came to see slavery as part of the world's great evil. When he was nineteen, he heard Rev. Samuel Hopkins, a famous antislavery preacher from Rhode Island, declare slavery to be "a great sin." "From this time," Owen wrote when an old man, "I was antislavery, as much as I be now."

Owen, and John Brown after him, believed that God had endowed mankind with an inalienable right to freedom. In this respect both men viewed the religious message of the Bible and the political message of the Declaration of Independence as one and the same.

In 1805, five years after John was born, Owen and Ruth left Torrington and went west, joining thousands of others leaving New England's rocky soil and heading for the fertile lands of the Ohio valley. Owen bought a large tract in Hudson, Ohio. It was a township that had been founded by David Hudson of Goshen, Connecticut, who led a band of New England pioneers to settle there in 1799. Hudson was in the very heart of the "Western Reserve," a wilderness tract of about 6,000 square miles that lay along the southern shore of Lake Erie, directly west of the Ohio-Pennsylvania line. Settled primarily by Connecticut people, the Western Reserve was almost literally a New England colony in the heart of the Midwest; and in 1803 it entered the Union as part of the state of Ohio. (See map, page 44.) John Brown made his home on the Reserve from 1805 to 1846. During his residence there the Reserve became a main center of antislavery activity and of the woolgrowing industry. John Brown's life was to be linked intimately with both aspects of the Reserve's development.

Owen and Ruth worked hard to build themselves a cabin, clear the land, feed and clothe their children and start a tannery business. Things went well until 1808, when Ruth died in childbirth, her baby with her. Owen laid the two to rest in the Hudson cemetery; he was left alone with five small children. "The remembrance of this scene," he wrote years later, "makes me bleed now."

Owen soon married again, and John found himself one of the older boys in a growing family. The loss of his mother had been devastating for him, and he pined after her for years. He became a loner. He explored the forest for miles around his home, watching birds, finding nests, catching squirrels. He had a way with animals. Later in life, he made a name for himself as a breeder of cattle, sheep, and horses. In an emergency he would doctor not only animals, but people as well, and do it excellently. He also learned farming and leather tanning from his father and prided himself on being a cattle driver. "To be sent off through the wilderness to very considerable distances," as he said of himself in a biographical sketch composed two years before Harper's Ferry, "was particularly his delight; and in this he was often indulged so that by the time he was twelve years old he was sent off more than a hundred miles with companies of cattle."

There was little provision for schooling on the frontier in those days. Children were lucky just to learn reading and writing. Brown attended a frontier school and dreamed of attending an eastern seminary and becoming a minister, but it never worked out. He "did not become much of a scholar," as he himself put it. He had to be content to stay home and work hard. He never learned to dance, though he loved to sing. He never gambled or played cards, preferred water to tea, and rarely touched liquor. He was a young man who kept his thoughts to himself and tackled whatever he set his hand to with deadly seriousness.

In 1814 he went to work at his father's tannery, much of the time acting as the supervisor of Owen's workers. The job suited him well; he seemed born to give commands and expected to be obeyed. This quality he combined with an extraordinary power to persuade others to follow him blindly. Milton Lusk, who attended school with Brown on the frontier, remembered "what a commanding disposition he always had." "There was such force and mastery in what he did," said Milton, "that everything gave way before him." But he was not good at listening to others. His "imperious or dictating way," as Brown himself described it, was a trait that would have drastic consequences later in his life.

In his youth, Brown's self-assuredness served him well. In 1819 he built a log cabin about a mile from his father's home, began building his own tannery, and went into business for himself. The widow Lusk, Milton's mother, kept house for him with the help, at times, of her eighteen-year-old daughter, Dianthe. Dianthe had her own special hiding place in the woods where she would go alone to pray. Sometimes she took Milton along to share her prayers. John described her as a "remarkably plain but neat, industrious and economical girl, of excellent character and remarkable piety." She sang beautifully.

The two married in 1820. For twelve years they shared the labors of making a home and raising a family. Dianthe bore seven children, five of whom survived: four sons, John Jr., Jason, Owen, Frederick; and one daughter, Ruth.

In 1825 John and Dianthe decided to move to Randolph township in western Pennsylvania, just across the state line from the Western Reserve, near Meadville. Randolph was at the time a largely unsettled wilderness. Bears prowled the woods and flocks of deer grazed in the underbrush. "I have listened both in my father's house and in the house of old John Brown," one of the neighbors recalled, "to the long howl of the wolf as he prowled about the sheepfolds and the barns in the darkness of the night."

Brown's ambition in Randolph was to build a big tannery, clear a large farm, and lay the foundations for his family's prosperity. He hired workers and threw himself with tremendous energy and enthusiasm into building his home and business—raising a house and a barn, digging tannery foundations and hauling in the stone, clearing the forest and planting crops. He was the first person to keep purebred animals in Crawford county, and had a large flock of sheep and fine Devon cattle.

Brown's spacious home was a double log cabin, with two big rooms on the ground floor and sleeping quarters for the children in the loft above. Husband and wife, children, and tannery workers—totaling at times as many as fifteen people—sat down at meals together. Day began with breakfast, and this was followed by a religious service. In the long winter evenings, when the day's work was done, all would gather in front of a blazing log fire. John Brown would begin a conversation on a topic of his own choice; the discussion might go on for hours. He liked to read from Benjamin Franklin's *Poor Richard* or Aesop's *Fables*. He was always ready to tell a story and point a moral. "God helps those who help themselves," he told his children. Whatever work you do, he told them, make sure that it is perfect to the last detail, for "a small leak will sink a great ship."

Soon Brown was a leading figure in the community. He surveyed land for the building of roads, built schoolhouses, found ministers to come and preach, and served as postmaster. He delighted, evidently, as one of his tannery workers, James Foreman, later phrased it, "to improve and help subdue the country, and grow up with the improvements made." If local people wished to praise someone highly they might call him "as enterprising and honest as John Brown."

In 1832 tragedy overtook the family. Dianthe died in childbirth, her baby with her. "Last night," Brown wrote his father, "my affectionate, dutiful and faithful Dianthe bade 'farewell to earth.' . . . At her request the children were brought to her and she with heavenly composure gave faithful advice to each." The grave may still be seen in a field behind the house; it bears the inscription, "farewell earth."

Like John Brown's own mother, Dianthe died young. Both women gave birth to seven children, of whom five survived, over twelve years of married life. This experience was typical for working women of that day. Unending work in the home and around the farm, numerous children to bear and to raise, high infant mortality, and the danger of death in childbirth—this was the harsh reality facing country women in early America.

John Brown was left with five young children to care for. He was a stern father who would not hesitate to spank children for small faults, like telling a fib, being too noisy or not doing what they were told. Strictness with children was common in those days, but Brown was probably stricter than most. Traditionalists like him believed that sin is "original" in mankind—that all people were born with this taint, laid upon them by God as punishment for disobedience in the Garden of Eden. Children were thought of as natural sinners. They couldn't do the right thing unless somebody was always after them.

Sometimes Brown's children saw tears in his eyes as he punished them. Ruth Brown, who was three and a half when Dianthe died, thought of her father as stern and tender at the same time. She remembered the day that he took her to be baptized, carrying her in his arms through the woods. A minister "put water on my face." Brown wiped the drops away "with a brown silk handkerchief with yellow spots on it in diamond shape. . . . I thought how good he was to wipe my face with that pretty handkerchief." Small touches such as this showed Ruth that her father loved her, and she loved him in return. "His tenderness," she wrote, "made me forget that he was stern."

The children also witnessed Brown's many kindnesses to neighbors, his tannery workers, and strangers. He urged his children to follow the Bible's teaching about the duty of hospitality to strangers. "Forget not to entertain strangers," he would read aloud, "for thereby some have entertained angels unawares."

Jason, Brown's second son, remembered how every year the Native American people used to come to Randolph from New York in the winter, and set up camp east of town so that they might hunt. "They often came to our house for food and hay for their ponies," Jason remembered. Some of the Randolph people didn't like this; and one Sunday they came with their guns to ask John Brown and his hired men to help them drive the Native Americans away. He refused, saying: "I will have nothing to do with so mean an act. I would sooner take my gun and help drive *you* out of the country." This, Jason remembered, was one of the first times that he saw his father get really mad.

Many of the strangers Brown took into his home throughout his life and helped in whatever way he could were fugitive slaves. He considered it, as James Foreman put it, "as much his duty to help a Negro make his escape as it was to help catch a horse thief." Black people fleeing the South crossed the Ohio River to Illinois, Indiana, or Ohio, hiding away on steamboats, swimming the broad river, or going over on foot on the winter ice. But their troubles were not over when they landed on free soil. The United States Constitution decreed that fugitives must be surrendered when their owners came to demand them. Even after they reached the North, therefore, runaway slaves lived in daily terror of being fingered by informers who wanted to earn a fat reward, or being hunted like wild animals by mounted slave catchers armed with pistols and accompanied by packs of dogs.

Throughout the North, antislavery people helped the fugitives to reach Canada, where the slave hunters could not get them. They hid them in back rooms and barns, fed and sheltered them until the pursuers had passed. They gave them clothes when, as often happened, they were in rags, and nursed them when they were sick. They hid them in wagons and hauled them from one hiding place to the next. People doing this work were in danger of severe punishment if they were caught, but most of them thought of what they did as simply a Christian duty. The black runaways were oppressed people fleeing tyrants; since when, it was asked, had Christians denied the right of sanctuary to the children of God?

Brown's eldest son, John Jr., had never seen a black before when a fugitive couple came to his father's door one winter night early in 1825. The four year old was curious: If you touched them, he thought to himself, the color would surely rub off. Then the woman, John Jr. wrote,

> took me up on her knee and kissed me. . . . Mother gave the poor creatures some supper; but they thought themselves pursued, and were uneasy. Presently father heard the trampling of horses crossing a bridge on one of the main roads, half a mile off; so he took his guests out the back door and down into the swamp near the brook to hide, giving them arms to defend themselves, but returning to the house to await the event. It proved a false alarm. . . . He brought them into the house again, sheltered them and sent them on their way.

At the age of twenty-five John Brown was not merely sheltering fugitives but also arming them, so that they could fight their hunters. In years to come he would dream of arming not merely a handful of fugitives but thousands of them.

4

JOHN BROWN'S OATH
Business and Anti-Slavery in the Western Reserve, 1833-43

In the summer of 1833, John Brown married for a second time. Mary Anne Day, aged sixteen, was the daughter of a blacksmith from the township of Troy; she was one of two sisters whom Brown hired early that year to run his house, care for his children, and feed his tannery workers. Mary lived with him until his death in 1859, bore thirteen sons and daughters, and survived him by twenty-five years. She was a large, powerfully built woman who worked hard, suffered much, and endured. Salmon, her third child, spoke of his mother "worn by child-bearing and child-rearing," and of his father "hovering over her night and day" during her frequent and often lengthy bouts of sickness.

Brown was often away on his travels, sometimes taking the older boys with him. For weeks, months and even years Mary and the remaining children were on their own. She was as dedicated to the antislavery cause as her husband, even after it had claimed his life and the lives of two of her three grown sons, Oliver and Watson.

Mary knew tragedy long before Harper's Ferry. Of her thirteen babies only six survived childhood—Anne, Sarah and Ellen, Watson, Salmon and Oliver. When she became a widow in 1859, nine of the thirteen were in their graves. She had survived years of endless toil for her family, as she herself said, only to preside "over the ruin of my house."

Mary's first child, Sarah, was born at Randolph in the spring of 1834. Before the baby was a year old John Brown moved back to the Western Reserve in Ohio to Franklin Township, which was only six miles from Hudson. For the next twenty years, until 1855, the Browns made the Western Reserve their principal home, living on farms which were only a few miles apart: first at Franklin and Hudson, then at Richfield, and finally at Akron. (See map, facing page 45.)

John Brown's return to Ohio coincided with a period of reckless growth in the nation's economy. During these early years of the 19th century the North was passing through the first phase of the Industrial Revolution. Products like shoes or clothes that people previously made at home or in the craftsman's shop were, quite literally, being taken out of their hands, and the manufacture of them was being given to machines. These machines were being brought together in big brick or wooden sheds called *manufactories*, a word which in the course of time was shortened to *factories*. The machines were driven, not by human or animal power, as had been most often the case before, but by water or steam. Little industrial towns with red brick factories and clusters of workers' houses were starting to spring up in southern New England, New York, New Jersey, and Pennsylvania. Workers came not only from the American countryside but from Europe, too, especially the British Isles. Every year these towns became larger and grimier.

Almost at once the Midwest began to feel the impact of these industrial changes. Pioneers and farmers moving west, like Owen Brown, had need of the new products which the factories were starting to supply—guns, clocks, axes, ploughs, kettles, and clothing. Midwesterners were a rapidly growing market for all these goods: in return, they could provide the food and raw materials needed in the East.

During the 1830's and 1840's, therefore, midwestern farmers were being drawn into producing crops, not just for their own personal consumption but for sale upon the market. This was a big change: it could never have taken place without the growth of a transportation system linking the eastern

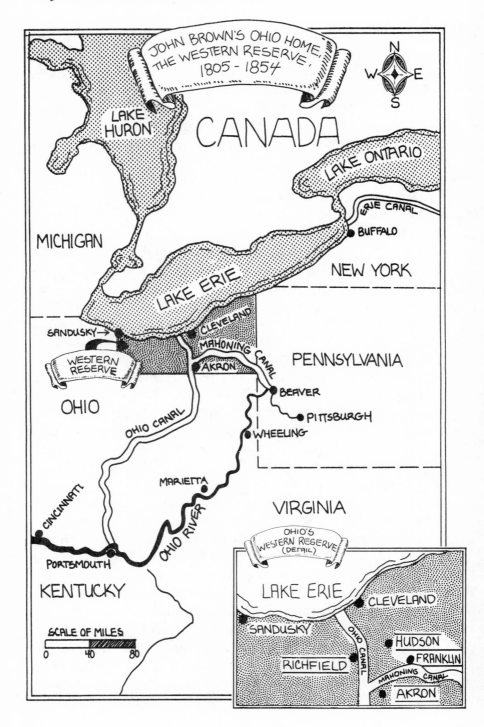

factory centers with western lands. Without roads, cattle trails, railroads, waterways, boats, bridges, and canals, food supplies and raw materials could not have been shipped east; finished products, in turn, could not have been shipped across the Appalachian mountain barrier to the West.

The building of the Erie Canal, linking the Midwest with New York City and the Atlantic Ocean, was an early transportation breakthrough. The Erie Canal, 364 miles in length, stretched from Buffalo on Lake Erie to Albany on the Hudson River. Irish immigrants wielding picks and shovels did most of the digging. They worked up to their knees in muck, half naked, with flannel shirts upon their backs and slouch caps upon their heads. Hundreds died in blasting accidents, of fever, sunstroke, and exhaustion. But after nine years of this labor the ditch was dug and filled with water. The canal opened for business along its full route in 1825.

The building of the Erie Canal marked the onset of rapid changes in midwestern economic life. New towns sprang up to import products from the East and to export farm goods from the West. The completion of the Erie Canal, too, launched a general boom in canal building; speculators began to buy up land and to project "feeder" canals along which produce might be sent from the Ohio countryside to the Erie waterway itself. All of this new construction brought about rising prices for land upon which new commercial centers might be built or upon which big crops might be raised for distant markets. People who bought up such lands fast, while the price was still low, could unload their property later on for double or triple what they had paid for it; in this way they could make fortunes.

The lure of big money from this speculative business drew John Brown back to the Western Reserve in 1835. He was, to be sure, a leading person in Randolph—a respected business-man, postmaster, employer of tannery workers. For John Brown, who wanted to make it big, this wasn't big enough. When he moved to Franklin the construction of the Mahoning Canal was about to begin. Running east and west this canal would not only link up the Western Reserve with the Erie

Canal and New York, but with Pittsburgh and Pennsylvania as well. Franklin, later named Kent, was upon the projected route of the Mahoning Canal. (See map, facing page 45.)

As soon as he had moved, Brown built himself a new tannery, and began to borrow money. He bought Frederick Haymaker's farm and other lands in the little village of Franklin Mills, a farm named Westlands that lay not far from Hudson, and yet another farm in Hudson Township itself. Just like other speculators, he dreamed of selling off these properties at a fat profit when land prices started to rise, when Franklin began to grow from sleepy frontier village to flourishing business center.

These rosy visions of easy wealth soon faded. In 1836 the federal government announced that it would no longer accept paper money issued by state banks for the purchase of federally owned lands—from now on, that is, people would have to buy such lands with hard cash, with gold or silver. Overnight the currencies of local banks became worthless, and the banks closed their doors. Worse was to follow: by 1837 business depression hit the North and the West. Jobless workers poured out onto the streets; in the Western Reserve the construction of the Mahoning Canal came to a stop. Many speculators holding near-worthless lands and with big debts to pay, faced bankruptcy. John Brown was among them.

In the years from Dianthe's death to the big collapse of 1837, John Brown was pretty much taken up with his own personal affairs. But during these same years the Western Reserve, with Hudson at its center, became a stronghold of the movement for the abolition of slavery.

It began on July 4, 1829, when a young man, twenty-four years old, rose to speak in a Boston meeting house. His name was William Lloyd Garrison, and he was a printer by trade. He was about to leave New England and go to Baltimore, to take up a job as editor of an antislavery newspaper.

Americans, said the young guest-lecturer, faced a crisis which threatened to destroy their free republic and to lay it in ruins. The crisis was caused by the existence of human slavery in a land dedicated to freedom. Two million men, women,

A Canalboat Moving through a Lock in the Erie Canal

Giant locks had to be constructed along the Erie Canal to enable boats to be lifted or lowered from one water level to another. One of the greatest of these lock systems was at Lockport, N.Y. This lithograph illustrates the massiveness of the construction involved. A special waterproof cement was invented and used in building such locks.
—Colden, Memoirs on the Opening of the Erie Canal, *1825.*

and children were being held in chains in the South, but white Americans, he charged, were indifferent: "scarcely an eye weeps, or a heart melts, or a tongue pleads either to God or man." This tyranny, growing by leaps and bounds, trampled not only upon blacks, but threatened the liberty of all Americans. The remedy was to grant the slaves their birthright of freedom as promised by the Declaration of Independence and the Bill of Rights. "Born upon our soil," he said, "they are entitled to all the privileges of American citizens. This is their country by birth, not adoption. Their children possess the same inherent and inalienable rights as ours; and it is a crime of the blackest dye to load them with fetters."

Soon Garrison was spreading his message of equal rights for blacks as American citizens far and wide with the help of the *Liberator,* a weekly paper that he launched from Boston in 1831. In the years that followed, John Brown learned much about antislavery struggles in the North and South from its pages.

During the 1830s antislavery societies began to spring up like mushrooms in New England, the mid-Atlantic states and the Midwest. Organizers traveled from town to town talking about the evils of slavery and inspiring the formation of new groups wherever they went. These societies found plenty to do. They demanded an end to segregation in public schools and public transportation. They flooded Congress with petitions to end the slave trade in Washington, D.C. They provided lawyers for black people accused of being fugitive slaves; they helped smuggle runaways to safety in Canada. They edited antislavery newspapers and wrote books about the slavery experience and its horrors.

As this movement grew and spread, its outlandish doctrines aroused fear and anger among whites, both North and South, who had no love for blacks and rejected with indignation the idea that blacks were equal to whites. Wherever antislavery leaders went to hold meetings and to give out literature they had to face mob violence. The lecture trails were marked by storms of hoots and jeers, a hail of rocks, bloody faces and splintered windows, smashed newspaper presses, the sound of blows, and, even, death.

If, during those years, Brown was preoccupied with his personal affairs, his concern about black people and their freedom had not died. In 1834 he wrote to his brother Frederick, who lived in Hudson, and voiced optimism that God would soon bring the black people "out of the house of bondage." He and Mary thought they could help them to freedom by adopting a slave child whom they would rear as their own. Better yet, they might start a school for blacks, perhaps in their own house. "Such a school," he wrote, "might do more in that way to break their yoke effectually than any other."

For Brown, who believed that to deny the equal rights of all people was to deny a fundamental truth of God, discrimination in church was particularly wicked. A little while later—it was probably in 1836—an incident occurred which showed how deeply he felt about this. As Ruth remembered the incident, her father hired a black couple to work for him at Franklin—the man on the farm and the woman in the house. "One Sunday," Ruth recalled, "the woman went to church, and was seated near the door or somewhere back." It was, indeed, the common practice in most Northern communities to admit black people to church, but to make them sit at the back, or in the gallery above. "This," said Ruth, "aroused father's indignation at once." Next Sunday both the man and his wife went with the Browns to church; John Brown marched them in and seated them in the family pew. "The whole congregation," Ruth remembered, "was shocked; the minister looked angry; but I remember father's firm, determined look."

The following year, in 1837, John Brown linked himself formally with the abolitionist movement and took the first step along the path that was to lead him, over twenty years later, to Harper's Ferry.

The Brown family, at that time, was living on the farm in Hudson Township. Mary's third child, Salmon, was born there in 1836. Among Salmon's earliest memories was the large house, and near it a huge rock out of which the spring water gushed cold and fresh. He wrote:

> In a large living room was a fireplace ten feet long, with huge andirons and a crane and hooks to hang kettles upon. We boys would cut logs two and three feet through for the fireplace, and at night, in winter, two great back-logs were covered with ashes to hold fire. Father would sit in front of a lively fire and take up us children one, two, or three at a time, and sing until bedtime. We all loved to hear him sing as well as talk of the conditions in the country, over which he seemed worried. A favorite song with father and us children was "Blow Ye the Trumpet, Blow."

One day in November 1837 Laurence Hickok came riding up to the house upon his horse. Hickok was professor of theology at Hudson's Western Reserve College, which Owen Brown had help to found, and he was a distinguished preacher and a writer. Hickok told the Browns that next day there would be an important meeting at the Congregational Church, and everybody was urged to attend. Then he rode off.

John Brown went to that meeting, which was crowded with townsfolk and with students from the college. Owen Brown was in the chair, and presided over the gathering.

Professor Hickok was the main speaker. In an angry, eloquent speech, he told the audience that Rev. Elijah Lovejoy, a Presbyterian minister, had been killed by a proslavery mob at Alton, Illinois.

Elijah Lovejoy was born and raised in the state of Maine; thirty-five years old at the time of his death in 1837, he was just two years younger than John Brown himself. Lovejoy graduated from Waterville (now Colby) College in 1826 at the top of his class, and went on to theology school. Like many young people at that time, he was captivated by the beauty of the West and the challenge of building a new life there. Resolving to become a minister he settled at St. Louis, Missouri. His main thought was to run a church and spread the word of God.

In 1834 an agent from the American Antislavery Society visited Lovejoy, and converted him to the antislavery cause. Soon Lovejoy's church paper, the St. Louis *Observer*, began to denounce slavery as a sin and as a cruel form of oppression. White leaders in St. Louis were furious, and they incited the community to anger, too. Twice in the summer of 1836 a mob invaded Lovejoy's office and wrecked it. He was driven from town and fled with his wife, Celia, and their small son to Alton, Illinois. It was a small town on a bluff overlooking the Mississippi River. "Surely," Lovejoy told himself, "I shall be able to continue my antislavery work in the free state of Illinois."

Lovejoy's hope was in vain. Three times from July 1836 to August 1837 mobs broke into his office, scattered his type, and dumped his press into the river. Three times Lovejoy made good the damage. Finally, at the end of October 1837, the conservative leadership of Alton lost patience. They called upon Lovejoy to stop preaching and writing his inflammatory antislavery doctrines, and to resign the editorship of the *Observer*. Only under these conditions, they warned, would he be permitted to go on living at Alton.

Lovejoy's fourth press was already on its way to town. "A voice," he told the townspeople of Alton, "calls upon me in the name of all that is dear in heaven or earth, to stand fast; and by the help of God, *I will stand.* I know I am but one and you are many. You can crush me if you will, but I shall die at my post, for I cannot and will not forsake it. I, and I alone, can disgrace myself; and the deepest of disgraces would be, at a time like this, to deny my Master by forsaking his cause."

On November 6 Lovejoy's fourth press arrived by boat from St. Louis; he and his friends unloaded it at the river dock, stored it in a warehouse, and posted armed guards. Within 24 hours the mob attacked and a pitched battle took place. Lovejoy, gun in hand, was killed amid a hail of bullets.

Such was the story that Laurence Hickok reported to the Hudson community. He finished by telling his audience—just as Garrison had told the Boston people in 1829—that the struggle at Alton involved not only the fate of the black people but the survival of the American republic itself. "The crisis has come," he said, "the question now before the American citizen is no longer alone 'can the slaves be made free?' but 'are *we* free or are *we* slaves under Southern mob law?'"

The afternoon wore on; speech followed speech; resolutions were passed. John Brown sat silent.

Just as Owen Brown was about to declare the meeting at an end, John Brown stood up, and raised his right hand. "Here, before God," he said, "in the presence of these witnesses, I consecrate my life to the destruction of slavery." Then Owen, in tears and without a trace of stammer, uttered a prayer for Lovejoy and for freedom, and brought the gathering to a close.

John Brown was not content to commit just himself to the antislavery cause. He sought to involve his family as well. John Brown, Jr. remembered how his father called them together one evening in 1838 or 1839: Mary, John Jr., Jason,

and Owen. Brown talked at length about the sufferings and
wrongs inflicted upon the slaves, and he asked, John Jr.
remembered, "who of us were willing to make common
cause with him, in doing all in our power 'to break the jaws of
the wicked, and pluck the spoil out of his teeth.'" He put the
same question to each of them in turn: "Are you, Mary? Are
you, John? Are you, Jason? Are you, Owen?" Each of them in
turn answered, "yes." Then John Brown asked them to raise
their hands and to swear to the same oath that he had himself
taken, that they would devote their lives to the struggle
against slavery.

John Brown's oath to commit his life to the destruction of
slavery may have sounded impressive but it had little meaning
at the time that he made it. There was no way, indeed, that he
could even begin to put his promise into practical effect.
When he rose to his feet in Hudson's Congregational Church
he was head over heels in debt. His creditors had already
begun to file suits against him to recover the money that he
owed them for all the lands that he had bought but not paid
for, and he had no funds at all with which to liquidate his
obligations. During 1838 and 1839 he launched frantic efforts
to borrow money and to avoid the foreclosure of his farms.
He was away from home for many months, driving cattle to
eastern markets and seeking to obtain loans from eastern
bankers.

John Brown drove his cattle over the six-hundred-mile trail
from Ohio to Connecticut, on a path that took him
northward to Erie, Pennsylvania, and then clear across New
York State to Albany. Great American cattle drives are usually
associated with the period after the Civil War, when cowboys
drove the longhorns northward from Texas to the railheads of
Kansas. Trail driving over huge distances had, in truth, begun
long before; Brown was one of many who followed the trails
from the Midwest to the east, across New York or
Pennsylvania, in the early part of the 19th century. He was
"not particularly graceful on horseback," his sons
remembered, "but it was very hard to throw him." John
Brown, indeed, loved animals, and he had an especial place in

his heart for horses. The very year that he took his oath at Hudson, he was breeding horses for the racecourse at Warren, a town on the Mahoning Canal some thirty miles east of Franklin.

Brown made no money in the East from the sale of his cattle, and he failed to get the loans he so urgently needed. Even worse, he took money advanced to him by the New England Woolen Company to buy wool for them in 1839, and used it to to pay pressing debts. When he set out for home from Connecticut in June 1839 all his efforts to stave off bankruptcy had ended in failure; he began to prepare Mary and the children for the grim future. "I have left no stone un-turned," he wrote to her, "to place my affairs in a more settled and comfortable shape, and now should I, after all my sacrifice of body and mind, be compelled to return a very poor man, how would my family receive me?"

The following year Brown lost the Haymaker farm at Franklin with its precious farm equipment and fine Saxony sheep; and then he lost Westlands, in the town adjoining Hudson. That same year he made a trip to western Virginia with the thought of settling there, but this project came to nothing. The next year, 1841, Brown went to work for one of his creditors, Heman Oviatt, as a shepherd on Oviatt's farm at Richfield, about ten miles to the west of Hudson. Salmon, six years old when the family moved to Richfield in 1842, described their new home as "an old whitewashed log house, with a mill pond and creek dam, with mud-turtles, which we boys would fatten and eat." He remembered his father at this time as "slightly stoop-shouldered after middle life, with eyes sky blue, hair dark brown . . . nose hawked and thin, skin florid, spare but muscular build. He wore boots, as was the custom in those days, and white shirts with a plait on each side of the bosom."

That same year, 1842, the United States court declared Brown to be bankrupt—a person, that is, who, having been stripped of his property, was no longer liable for the full amount of all his debts outstanding. The Hudson farm where Salmon Brown had been born along with his two little brothers, Charles and Peter, was sold at public auction. All John Brown's farms had now gone, and most of his personal property as well, the proceeds from sale being divided among the creditors. All that remained to the Brown family were their beds and blankets, cups, saucers, and spoons, a washtub and a couple of earthen crocks, some food for the winter—like potatoes, corn, beans, apples, and pork—some farm animals, and a variety of tools like hoes and sheep shears.

Deeper sorrow followed. In September 1843, when they had been living at Richfield for little more than a year, four of the children died within a few days of each other after they became ill with dysentery. First Charles died, a little boy of six years, "very swift and strong," as his brother Salmon described him, "his legs and arms straight as broomsticks, of sandy complexion, quiet as a cat, but brave as a tiger." Then Austin, the newborn baby, died; then Peter, aged three, born at Hudson in 1840, "very strong, darker than Charles, the best-looking member of the family." Last of all died Sarah, Mary's first-born; the child was nine.

"Four of our number sleep in the dust, and were all buried together in one grave," wrote the heartbroken father to John Jr. "This has been a bitter cup to all of us indeed, and we have drunk deeply. . . . Sarah during her sickness discovered great composure of mind, and patience, together with a strong assurance at times of meeting God in Paradise. We fondly hope that she is not disappointed."

5

IS MY SHEEP BRUNG IN?
From the Western Reserve to
Springfield, Massachusetts, 1844-47

> The master of the sheepfold bin
> He wants to know,
> *Is my sheep brung in?*
> —Shepherd's Song, New England

When John Brown was declared bankrupt in 1842 he was allowed to retain, along with clothes, household effects, and farm tools, "19 sheep pledged to H. Oviatt." Evidently he paid the debt that he owed to Oviatt in labor; those nineteen sheep, or some of them, were the beginning of a flock that John Brown himself was building up.

The opening of the Mahoning Canal in 1840 spelled big economic changes that were soon to come to the Western Reserve; and these would, at least for a while, rescue the Brown family from its poverty. The Mahoning Canal was a waterway that Brown himself had worked upon in 1835, when he hauled fill and helped to dig the ditch. The canal ran from Akron, where it joined the Ohio Canal, through the Western Reserve, then down to Beaver on the Ohio River. There the Mahoning connected with the "main line" Pennsylvania–Ohio Canal that had been built from Pittsburgh to Philadelphia. (See map, page 44.) The opening of the Mahoning to traffic in 1840 was a big event. Taken together, the Ohio, Mahoning and Erie canals linked the Ohio heartland with the industrial East.

The immediate effect of the opening of the Mahoning in the Wesern Reserve was to boost the production of wool. In 1843, about 390,000 pounds of it were shipped from Cleveland, much of this from the Western Reserve. Eight years later, in 1851, this figure had risen to the staggering total of nearly four million pounds.

Brown's chance to benefit from this growing industry came in 1843, when he met a rich merchant, Simon Perkins, Jr., who had a sheep farm at the edge of Akron. Early in 1844 Perkins and Brown signed an agreement to go into the wool business together. Under this agreement the two men pooled their sheep and handled them as a single flock. Perkins paid the cost of food and shelter for the sheep during the winter months and provided the Browns with a nice house close by his own elegant mansion, with its graceful Southern-style portico. Brown and his family took care of the animals, sheared, sacked, and marketed the wool, according to the agreement, "in the neatest and best manner." Each partner was entitled to an equal share of the money that came in from the sale of wool.

John Brown was jubilant about this arrangement. "I have entered into a partnership with Simon Perkins, Jr., of Akron," he wrote to John Jr., "with a view to carry on the sheep business extensively. This is the most comfortable and the most favorable arrangement of my worldly concerns that I ever had . . . no mean alliance for the poor bankrupt and his family."

Early in 1844 John Brown went to work at Akron to build up a pedigree flock and to market wool perfectly clean, and high in quality. This Perkins-Brown flock soon won a reputation as, in the words of one wool producer, "the finest and most perfect flock of Saxon sheep in the United States." Here the secret of Brown's success lay not only in his talent as a handler and breeder of animals, but in the endless time and effort that he was prepared to devote to the job of raising the wool for market.

This is well illustrated by a manual that he wrote about cleaning and preparing wool, and published as a guide for the benefit of other American wool growers. First, he wrote, the wool must be thoroughly washed. "The best manner of washing," he said, "is to use a fall of three feet or over, turning the sheep in different ways under the fall, till the action of the fall brings every part of the fleece to a snowy whiteness." If no waterfall was available, "a clear running stream should be found, and the dirt worked out perfectly from all parts of the fleece with the hands. . . ."

Following these instructions produced beautifully clean wool; it also demanded much effort. When John Brown and his sons washed sheep in this way they had to stand for hours at a time in cold water, bent double as they held the sheep in the stream, soaked the wool, then squeezed, and scrubbed, and rinsed.

As soon as the sheep were thoroughly dry, Brown continued, they must be sheared in a sheepfold—that is, an enclosed space or bin, well littered with straw to prevent contamination of the wool by sheep droppings. Once the fleeces had been taken off, "they should be minutely gone over by hand to detect and remove every burr they might contain." With a large flock and a big wool harvest, this last operation alone required many hours of patient work.

Brown devoted the same attention to the care of his flock as he did to the preparation and cleaning of the wool. One spring, his daughter, Ruth, recalled, the ewes had "grub in the head," a disease which made it impossible for them to recognize their own lambs and give them suck. "For two weeks," said Ruth, "Father did not go to bed, but sat up or slept an hour or two at a time in his chair, and then would take a lantern, go out and catch the ewes, and hold them while the lambs sucked."

Sometimes the newborn lambs were in danger of freezing to death when the weather was unusually cold. "He would often," Ruth remembered, "bring in a little dead-looking lamb, and put it in warm water and rub it until it showed signs of life, and then wrap it in a warm blanket, feed it warm milk with a teaspoon, and work over it with such tenderness that in a few hours it would be capering around the room."

One of John Brown's favorite sayings from the Bible was "a righteous man regardeth the life of his beast." His success with animals was due in great part to the fact that he had a genuine feeling for them, and loved nothing more than to take care of them. This made it possible for him to commit himself to every detail of a shepherd's work with an enthusiasm that other Ohio farmers did not necessarily share.

During 1844 and 1845 Brown traveled widely throughout the Ohio Valley region in order to buy sheep. As he drove along the road with his light team, he might spot a flock of sheep grazing on the hillside. He would stop and visit with the farmer, and be invited to dinner. Conversation about sheep and sheepraising would last far into the night; the next day John Brown would go on his way. Through these travels and visits during the early 1840's, he came to know hundreds of sheep farmers in the Ohio Valley region, including many people in the hilly or western portion of Virginia.

The sheepraisers whom he met, and whose hospitality he shared, talked readily enough about their problems: Eastern manufacturers who bought their wool were paying prices that were too low. Brown suggested a remedy that he put forward both in private conversations and at woolgrowers' meetings. Not only, said he, must the wool be thoroughly cleansed before being sent to market; it must also be graded. What the woolgrowers needed to do, he proposed, was to set up a cooperative enterprise, where the wool could be collected, sorted into different grades according to quality, then sold to the manufacturers at a price representing its true market value. Such a cooperative, too, could withhold wool from the market when the going price was too low, and sell in larger quantities when the price was high.

To clean and grade wool properly and market it cooperatively seemed like elementary common sense to John Brown. During the Middle Ages, centuries earlier, English monks, especially the Cistercians, raised sheep by the tens of thousands on England's moors and downs, and they followed the same practices that John Brown was advocating. They cleaned, graded, and marketed their wool so well that it long held the dominant place in Western Europe's wool market.

Some of Ohio's farmers were impressed by Brown's advice. By the mid-1840's he and Simon Perkins had the reputation of being among the best woolgrowers in the West, and nobody sold their fleeces at a higher price. Agreeing to his proposal, the farmers suggested that Brown himself undertake the job of organizing and running the seller's cooperative that he had talked about.

Brown then took his plan to Simon Perkins and persuaded his partner to go along with this idea. Early in 1846 an announcement of the new venture was prepared; copies were sent to farmers in northern Ohio, western Pennsylvania and Virginia, and New York. Perkins and Brown gave notice that they had set themselves up in business as wool merchants and wool graders in order "to receive wool from growers . . . and to sell the same for cash at its real value, when quality and condition are considered." They would store and grade the wool received, provide cash advances before sale, then sell to dealers and manufacturers. Each farmer would be charged two cents a pound commission, with a small fee for postage and insurance.

In order to launch this new business it was agreed that Brown would go east and, with the help of John Jr., establish a center for the storage and sale of wool at Springfield, Massachusetts. Jason and Owen Brown would remain at Akron with the family and take charge of the Perkins-Brown flock.

Jason and Owen were, like John Jr., the sons of Dianthe; all three men were experienced farmers in their early twenties. Mary, with a family of young children to care for, remained for the time being at Akron. She now had three little boys—Watson, Salmon, and Oliver—a daughter, Annie, aged three, and a newborn child, Amelia. By the time that her husband was ready to leave for Springfield in the summer of 1846, Mary was pregnant once more. The baby, Sarah, was born in Akron two months after her father had departed.

In July John Brown and John Jr. moved east, having rented half of an old warehouse in Springfield, close by the railroad line; and taking up living quarters in a little house close by. "There is no mistake about doing a vast business," Brown wrote to Perkins with easy confidence, *"and perfectly safe."* Soon he and John Jr. were up to their eyes in work—corresponding with woolgrowers and manufacturers, paying out cash advances for wool received, keeping accounts and grading fleeces.

Late in September came the happy news of Sarah's birth, followed soon by tragedy. Ruth, age seventeen, back from school in Austinberg, Ohio, to help Mary with the baby, by accident spilled scalding water over Amelia. The child died: "one more dear little feeble child," Brown lamented, when he heard the news, "I am no more to meet till all the dead, both small and great, shall stand before God." He was tormented by the pain of death and separation, by the thought that he was powerless to help Mary and the family when they most needed him. "If I had a right sense of my habitual neglect of my family's eternal interests," he wrote Mary, "I should probably go crazy."

The pain within his own family only heightened the torment Brown felt for the violence and the scattering of their families that slaves endured. In May 1846 he watched in horror as, following a skirmish between Mexican and American troops near the Rio Grande, Congress declared war against Mexico. War alone, said President James Polk in his message to Congress, could avenge "the honor, the rights, and the interests of our country." The House of Representatives agreed with him: They voted for war by 174 to 14. Joshua Giddings, a representative of the people of the Western Reserve, was one of the fourteen who voted "no." "The war is waged," he told the House, "for the purposes of conquest; with the design to extend slavery. . . ."

American soldiers marched off to war. An army under General Zachary Taylor thrust down the coast of Texas, crossed the Rio Grande, and invaded northern Mexico. Another army under Colonel Stephen Kearney headed southwest from Sante Fe to seize New Mexico and California. In February 1847 General Winfield Scott landed with fourteen thousand men at the Mexican port of Vera Cruz and moved inland to take Mexico City. By the second week of September, after bloody fighting, the struggle was over. Mexico surrendered a vast area, 850,000 square miles stretching from the Atlantic on the east to the Pacific on the west. Every inch of this territory, Southerners insisted, must be open to settlement by slaveholders. Had it not been conquered at the cost of Southern blood and Southern treasure?

John Brown drew his own conclusions from these events. The slave masters, evidently, not only ruled their slaves, but they had control of the federal government as well. The government, as the war showed, had become an instrument of conquest. How long, he asked himself, could free Americans survive if they failed to confront, and to cut down, this tyranny? Feelings of deep frustration possessed him. Ten years had now passed since he had made an oath, in the presence of God and his father, to give his life to the struggle to overthrow slavery in the United States. Over this time the menace of slavery had grown greater, not less. And here he was, sitting in a warehouse sorting wool!

These mingled, conflicting emotions were expressed in a letter that he wrote to Mary in March 1847, almost at the very moment that Winfield Scott was landing his invading army at Vera Cruz. "There is a peculiar music," he told her,

> in the word "home," which a half year's absence in a distant country [that is, Massachusetts] would enable you to understand. Millions there are who have no such thing to lay claim to. I feel considerable regret that I have lived so many years and have in reality done so little to increase the amount of human happiness.

The crisis of the Mexican War spurred Brown to move ahead with his plans for freeing the slaves. Knowing that the slaves themselves must accomplish their own liberation, he turned to Frederick Douglass for help and advice.

Frederick Douglass was a slave who fled from Maryland in 1838, settled in New England, and later purchased his freedom. Powerfully built, with a shock of black hair and a deep mellow voice, Douglass emerged as a public figure when he became an abolitionist speaker in 1841, inspiring audiences with the story of his life and his bold attacks upon slavery and all its works. His *Narrative of the Life of Frederick Douglass*, published in 1845, sold by the tens of thousands of copies in the United States and Great Britain. Douglass lived at Rochester, New York, where he was soon to publish an antislavery paper, *The North Star*, and was active in underground railroad work. When he came to visit Brown in 1847 at Springfield he was not yet thirty years old, but he was already known as one of America's foremost black leaders.

Douglass was born a slave in Talbot County, Maryland. He never knew his father; his mother, Harriet, was a slave woman. Harriet died when he was eight years old; he grew up as an orphan, left pretty much to his own devices. He ran errands, served as a bird-dog for one of the young masters, drove the cows in from pasture. He suffered not so much from overwork as from neglect. "I was kept almost naked," he wrote, "no shoes, no stockings, no jacket, no trousers, nothing but a coarse linen shirt, reaching only to my knees." Douglass, like the other half-naked slave youngsters growing up on the plantation, had no regular bed that he could call his own. In the cold weather he kept from freezing by stealing a bag used for sacking corn. "I would crawl into this bag," he said, and "there sleep on the cold, damp, clay floor, with my head in and my feet out."

The children were fed mostly on corn meal mush, set down in a trough outside the kitchen door. "They were called like so many pigs," Douglass remembered, "and like so many pigs would come, some with oyster shells, some with pieces of shingles, but none with spoons, and literally devour the mush."

When Frederick was a little older he was sent away to Baltimore, to be the slave of a child his own age, Thomas Auld. He soon understood that the road to freedom, for him, lay in learning how to read and write; he began his own battle to get an education. The neighborhood kids, who were always hungry, taught him how to spell, and in return he gave them bread which he stole from the Auld home. As for writing, he did not need paper. "My copybook," he wrote, "was the board fence, brick wall, and pavement; my pen was a lump of chalk."

Douglass now began to devour every book dealing with slavery that he could beg, borrow, or steal. By the age of twelve he understood that slaveholders "were a band of successful robbers, who had left their homes, and gone to Africa, and stolen us from our homes, and in a strange land reduced us to slavery." The desire for freedom became an obsession. He began to dream of fleeing North as "a possible means of gaining the liberty for which my heart panted."

After a few years in Baltimore Douglass was sent home to the plantation. Now he was no longer a child but a young man of fifteen years, angry and defiant. He was sent to work for a man called Covey; the sufferings that he endured seemed more like dream than reality. On a Sunday he would stand, gazing out across the broad Chesapeake Bay, watching the ships with their white sails as they moved toward the ocean. "You are free," he lamented, "I am a slave. You move merrily before the gentle gale, and I sadly before the bloody whip. . . . O that I were free!"

In 1838, when he was twenty, Douglass succeeded in making his way to New York, and then to New England. While living in Baltimore he had become a skilled shipbuilder; he hoped to earn his living practicing his craft at the whaling port of New Bedford in Massachusetts. But white workers refused to work alongside a black craftsman. Douglass had to be content with menial jobs, like shoveling coal, sweeping chimneys, and rolling oil casks.

When Frederick Douglass received John Brown's invitation to visit him in Springfield in the fall of 1848, he responded eagerly. Other black leaders had spoken to him, in words tinged with awe, about this white man who made no secret of his conviction that the slaves must win freedom with arms in

Frederick Douglass 1818–1895

This portrait of the famous black leader was made during his later years.
—Harper's Weekly, *1883*

hand. He found the Brown family inhabiting "a small, wooden building on a back street in a neighborhood of laboring men. . . . Plain as was the outside, the inside was plainer . . . no sofas, no cushions, no curtains, no carpets." Mary Brown and the children cooked and served up a meal of cabbage, potatoes, and beef soup. "They went through it as if used to it," said Douglass, "untouched by any thought of degradation or impropriety." He was amazed at this. White Americans, at that time, rarely invited black people to their homes as honored guests; they would have scorned to break bread with a black, or to wait upon him at table.

The meal finished, the boys cleared the table and washed the dishes. John Brown began to unfold his plan for the liberation of the slaves.

6

TO THE HILLS
Planning the Liberation of the Slaves, 1847–51

I will lift up mine eyes to the hills,
Whence cometh my salvation.
—One Hundred and Twenty-first
Psalm

Douglass studied his host closely. The man was lean and sinewy, "clad in plain American woolen, shod in boots of cowhide leather, and wearing a cravat of the same substantial material, under six feet high, less than one hundred and fifty pounds in weight, aged about fifty . . . straight and symmetrical as a mountain pine." His head was small, his hair coarse and strong; as he talked his clear gray eyes "alternated with tears and fire."

When John Brown met with Douglass, most abolitionists did not believe that armed struggle would be necessary to end slavery. Garrison believed that the most important thing to do was to strive to change American public opinion and to eliminate racist attitudes toward black people. Some abolitionists felt that it would be wise to reason with the slaveholders, convert them to antislavery views, and persuade them to give up their slaves of their own free will. This was Douglass' own opinion at the very time he was listening to Brown. Still other abolitionists—their leader was James G. Birney, who had himself once been a slaveholder in Alabama—thought that the most important thing to do was to organize an independent antislavery party which would win political power through the electoral process.

John Brown's ideas were different. He had little faith either in the power of persuasion or in political action. Slavery, Brown told Douglass, was a kind of war. From the very start, slaveholders had used violence to seize African people and to hold them down so that they could be worked to death for the benefit of whites. Day in and day out, he said, slave owners whipped, abused, terrorized, and murdered black people for the sake of money; the slaves fought back in whatever ways they could. Human nature, he told Douglass, was everywhere the same; wherever in the world people are ill-treated and abused they will feel the same pain and anger, the same will to resist, to rid themselves with their own hands of those who ruin their lives and steal their labor. "I am not averse to the shedding of blood," he said, "for no people can have self-respect who will not fight for their freedom."

John Brown was well informed about recent slave rebellions in the Americas. He was familiar with the tremendous revolt that Nat Turner organized in Virginia in 1831, which shook the slavery system to its foundations. He had followed the epic of the Spanish slaving ship, *Amistad*, that began in 1839 when African slaves rose up in bloody mutiny on the high seas and, under their leader, Cinque, began a two-year struggle that ended in freedom. He had, above all, become familiar with the story of Haiti. In 1791 tens of thousands of slaves had risen in revolt on that rich French sugar island and after years of brutal struggle had won their independence. Slavery in the United States, he told Douglass, would come to an end when black people themselves took up arms and did away with it.

The problem, as John Brown saw it in 1847, was how to help the slaves of the South fulfill their heart's desire; how to help them begin a struggle that would bring freedom in the end. At the outset Brown assured Douglass that he did not "contemplate a general rising of the slaves, and a general slaughter of the slave masters. . . ." Even after Harper's Ferry he went out of his way to repeat this statement and to underline it. "I never did intend," he said, "to incite slaves to rebellion, or to make insurrection." He had in mind, on the contrary, a plan of work which, conducted slowly and patiently over months and years, would one day bring freedom to the slaves. Shedding blood in an attack upon slaveholders and shedding blood in defense of freedom were, to John Brown, two quite different things.

How, then, to begin? By 1847 the Southern plantations, where a majority of the black people lived and worked, were scattered over a huge "black belt" stretching from the Atlantic coast hundreds of miles to the West. These were slave camps where masters and overseers kept watch by day, and military patrols, mounted and armed, went on the prowl by night. The slaves were pinned down on far-flung estates, and also split up; they were powerless to communicate, travel, organize or combine. A united, coordinated attack upon the slaveholders was all but impossible; for Brown the mere suggestion of such a thing was absurd.

The challenge, as John Brown saw it in 1847, was to find a way for the slaves to concentrate their forces and to build up strength. A map of the United States lay before him on the table; he indicated with his finger the ramparts of the Appalachian range that stretched from the heights of Maine southwest for some twelve hundred miles before petering out in the foothills of northern Alabama. In the South proper, the mountains ran right through Virginia, Kentucky, North Carolina, Tennessee, South Carolina, and Georgia. They were, Brown told Douglass, a stone dagger thrust into the heart of slavery's empire. "These mountains," Brown said, "are the basis of my plan. God has given the strength of freedom to these hills; they were placed there for the emancipation of your race."

He outlined three separate stages of his plan.

First, Brown proposed to place a very small force of armed men in the hills, positioning them in rocky hideaways, which he called "natural forts, where one man for defense will be equal to a hundred for attack." Again he stressed that he would start on a small scale, with squads of five men each, scattered along a twenty-five mile stretch of hills. These squads would quietly scour the countryside far and wide on both sides of the hills. They would seek recruits from amongst the boldest of the slaves, would explain to them the plan of action, would try to persuade them to flee the plantations and to cast in their lot with the mountain bands.

The second stage would begin, said Brown, when the original force had grown to a hundred men or more. The effort would now be made to attract large numbers of fugitives to the camps in the hills. The bravest and youngest of these people would be recruited to swell the ranks of the mountain army. Those who had no wish to stay and fight would be free, as fugitives always had been, to follow the mountain trail northwards. These fugitives would go in family groups—men and women with their families, old people and little children. Supplied with food, guards, and guides, they would now be able to move in larger numbers and with greater speed. What once had been a trickle would become a stream. The effect of the plan would soon be seen. "If," Brown told Douglass, "we could drive slavery out of one county, it would be a great gain." If slavery were made insecure anywhere in Virginia, this would weaken the institution throughout the state.

In the third stage of operations, as the mountain army grew larger and more experienced, it would enlarge the "zone of concentration" so that fugitives might be drawn to it, not just from one state, but from several. Growing success would eventually have an impact upon the entire South and upon the institution of slavery generally. Many owners would become anxious to rid themselves of so uncertain a type of property.

Douglass, as might be expected, had many questions and objections; the discussion continued far into the night. He pointed out that the slaveholders would under no conditions permit bodies of armed men to skulk in the hills and to threaten the survival of slavery itself. They would sniff out the rebels with bloodhounds, call in state and federal troops, surround the rebel strongholds, cut their supply lines, starve them out and destroy them.

Brown readily agreed that some squads might be surrounded and their men killed; but others, he insisted, might survive. Even if the entire operation proved a failure, he said, what of it? "I have no better use for my life, than to lay it down in the cause of the slave."

Why, Douglass asked Brown, did he think that force was necessary to bring slavery to an end? Why not start by trying to convert the slaveholders peacefully to abolitionism? Brown answered that such a thing was out of the question. Slaveholders were a class of people who had won power and profit through force and violence—by the seizure and exploitation of another class of people. They would not give up this power without a fight. "I know their proud hearts," he said.

John Brown told Douglass his dream. Twelve years before he went to Harper's Ferry John Brown had conceived a vision of struggle and of freedom which he viewed not merely as fantasy but, as Douglass put it, *"as divine command."* To find the ways to realize that dream would henceforth give meaning to Brown's existence. Douglass himself continued with his antislavery work, but began to lose faith in the idea that slavery could be abolished without armed struggle; the evening with John Brown had made a deep impression upon him.

During 1848 John Brown, with the help of John Brown, Jr., continued the endless work of receiving, sorting, grading and bagging wool. Wool prices that year were not as good as they had been in 1847, and the trend was downward. Brown, accordingly, held much of his supply from the market in the hope that prices would rise at least to the 1847 level, and that the wool producers, whose agent he was, would receive their fair reward. This was not at all to the liking of the producers, who needed cash right away so that they could pay their bills. They bombarded Brown with urgent pleas that he sell their fleeces. But Brown kept stubbornly to his policy of "no sale until the price is right," even though this caused problems for the wool growers. "It is painful," he wrote to one of these growers early in 1849, "that our friends are suffering for the proceeds of the wool before the right time to sell arrives."

Brown's thoughts in 1848 were far away from the dull routine and endless correspondence and account-keeping of his daily work. He had lifted up his eyes not only to the southern Appalachians but also to the Adirondack Mountains that lay beyond Lake Champlain far away to the northwest of his Springfield home. Only a few months after he had talked with Douglass he took the opportunity to move his family to the Adirondacks and to prepare himself and them for the mountain life and mountain struggle that he saw ahead.

In 1846 Gerrit Smith offered one hundred thousand acres of Adirondack wilderness that he owned to black people, fugitive slaves, or others who might undertake to clear land and turn it into farms. Gerrit Smith was the son and heir of Peter Smith, who had been a partner of John Jacob Astor in the fur trade. Both Smith and Astor had amassed fortunes from furs and from land speculation; they were among New York's first multimillionaires. Gerrit Smith inherited vast tracts of New York land. He lived at Peterboro, New York, at the western extremity of the Adirondacks, in a fine mansion on a large estate, and he gave lots of money to charitable causes.

In April 1848 John Brown went to Peterboro and visited Smith. He raised the possibility that he himself would take up some of the Adirondack lands that Smith was offering. Brown explained that he loved opening up the wilderness and building new communities; he didn't mind the hardships involved. He would not only start his own farm, with the help of his family, he told Smith; he would also employ black people and teach them the farming and pioneering skills which they needed. "I will be a kind of father to them," he said. The two men hit it off well. Smith shared Brown's antislavery convictions, and he was delighted at the idea of an experienced frontiersman working with his small black colony. The relationship between the two remained close until Harper's Ferry.

May 1848 was made happy by the birth of a daughter, Ellen. In September John Brown took Mary and Ellen to visit Mary's brother at Whitehall, New York, where he lived at the southernmost tip of Lake Champlain. Brown continued across the lake on a visit to the colony in the Adirondacks. The black community was located at North Elba, in Essex County. Ten families lived together in thickly forested hill country in a little huddle of cabins called Timbucto. Each family worked its own farm of 40 acres. The life was hard and rough, much like the life that John Brown had himself experienced when a child in the Western Reserve. The black pioneers had nothing except what they could produce themselves. The land was fine for raising cattle, pigs, sheep and vegetables. But the growing season was very short. Staple crops like corn and wheat did not thrive. Winter in the high hills with its deep snows endured for six months of the year, and the cold was arctic in intensity.

Difficulties such as these were nothing to John Brown. He saw here a challenge to work with the very same people who might one day be called upon to build a frontier community in the southern mountains, yes, and to fight there. What better place, he asked himself, for a poor man to settle? What better place for his children—Watson, Oliver, Salmon, Sarah, Ellen, and Annie—to grow up hardy, self-reliant and independent, even as he had done?

"I can think of no place where I would sooner go," he wrote to his father, "all things considered, than to live with these despised Africans, to try and encourage them and show them a little—so far as I am capable—of how to manage."

After visiting Timbucto John Brown went back to Whitehall, picked up Mary and Ellen and returned to Springfield. The trip home in the October weather was too much for the baby, and she caught a cold which soon turned into pneumonia. The first months of 1849 John Brown spent every moment that he could spare with Ellen, walking her up and down cradled in his arms, singing to her for hours on end. The baby waited for the sound of his footstep. "When she heard him coming up the steps to the door," Ruth remembered,

> she would reach out her little hands and cry for him to take her.
> When his business at the wool store crowded him so much that

he did not have time to take her, he would steal around through the woodshed into the kitchen to eat his dinner, and not go into the dining-room, where she could see and hear him. I used to be charmed myself with his singing to her.

One day, when he was leaving for the warehouse he noticed a change, and returned home for a special visit at noon. Bending over the cradle he whispered, "she is almost gone." Ellen opened her eyes and, as her sister Ruth described it, "put up her little wasted hands with such a pleading look for him to take her that he lifted her from the cradle . . . and carried her until she died." Then, very calmly, he closed the child's eyes, folded her hands upon her breast, and laid her back in the cradle. He comforted Mary, who was worn out with care and sorrow, and Ruth and the other children. But as he buried Ellen the next day, Ruth wrote, "he broke down completely, and sobbed like a child."

Three weeks later, in the middle of May, John Brown and his family put Springfield and its sad associations behind them and moved to North Elba. The main party was composed of John and Mary, Ruth, aged twenty, Oliver, aged ten, Annie and Sarah, aged six and three, respectively. John Jr., twenty-eight and the oldest of all the Brown children, remained behind at Springfield in charge of the wool business; Jason and Frederick remained in Ohio at the Simon Perkins farm, taking care of the Perkins-Brown sheep. As for Owen, Watson and Salmon, they had been sent off together to Connecticut with instructions to fetch some fine Devon cattle that their father had bought, and to drive them up to the farm in the mountains.

John Brown, Mary, Ruth, and the small children moved overland with the old farm wagon and their household goods. They came from Springfield over the Green Mountain trails, then descended through pastures on the western side of the hills where the sheep were grazing in huge flocks, to the little town of Burlington. There they crossed the broad waters of Lake Champlain to Westport on the New York side, where Brown bought a pair of fine horses to draw the wagon into the hills, and hired Thomas Jefferson, a black man, to be his teamster. Then they climbed up through the gorges of the Adirondacks, along the road to Keene. They drank water from streams that ran crystal clear over white sand and pebbles. After a day's travel from Westport they came to the Flanders farm that Brown had rented west of Keene. The house had one large room where the Browns cooked their food, ate their meals, and passed their time on winter nights. There was space in this room, too, for four of the family to sleep. Above the living room there were two smaller bedrooms. One other person shared these sleeping quarters with the Brown family. This was a young fugitive slave who had fled from Florida to Springfield, whom Brown had taken in, and who worked with the family on the farm. Brown also employed two other workers who lived in Timbucto: Thomas Jefferson, the teamster, and a housekeeper to help Mary.

To us today it may seem that the tiny Flanders house was very overcrowded with ten people sleeping under its roof. But Ruth assures us that "whenever a stranger or wayfaring man entered our gates, he was not turned away." Only two or three weeks after the Browns had themselves arrived at North Elba, three strangers did appear, ravenously hungry, and asked to be taken in. These were men from Boston on a walking tour, who had gotten lost in the trackless forest and nearly starved to death. One of them was Richard Henry Dana. He was a lawyer who fought for the rights of seafaring men and of fugitive slaves. He is famous, too, for his *Two Years Before the Mast*, an account of life at sea aboard a Yankee sailing ship.

Dana found the country around North Elba inexpressibly beautiful. "The Adirondack Mountains," he wrote,

> wave with woods, and are green with bushes, to their summits; torrents break down into the valleys on all sides; lakes of various sizes and shapes glitter in the landscape, . . . Tahawus [Mount Marcy or "Old White Face"], the highest peak, is about 5,400 feet high. . . . From John Brown's small log house, Old White Face, the only exception to the uniform green and brown and black hues of the Adirondack hills, stood plain in view, rising at the head of Lake Placid, . . ."

When Dana visited North Elba John Brown was busy marking boundary lines and surveying lands for the black pioneers and other farmers. Dana described him as "a tall, gaunt, dark-complexioned man, walking before his wagon, having his theodolite and other surveyor's instruments with him." He noted that Brown possessed a library of books, and that he made good use of them. As for the family, "he seemed to have an unlimited family of children, from a cheerful, nice, healthy woman of twenty or so [Ruth] and a full-sized red-haired son [Owen], through every grade of boy and girl to a couple [Annie, Sarah], that could hardly speak plain." Dana also observed what Frederick Douglass had recorded two years earlier—that the whole family sat down at table with the black workers, who were treated with great courtesy, and that Brown called them by their surnames, to which he added the prefixes of "Mr." or "Mrs." The meal, he added, "was neat, substantial and wholesome."

John Brown returned to his work at the warehouse in Springfield in July 1849, after the family was well settled into its new home; then he made preparations to sail for England. His last chance to save Perkins and Brown from collapse was to dump large quantities of unsold wool, and in particular the finer grades, on the English market.

In the first half of the 19th century the American South captured the European market for raw cotton. This was an historic achievement. The South, using slave labor, became the world's top producer of cotton. The rapid expansion of the slave empire was powered by the demand of Europe's textile factories for all the cotton that the United States could produce.

In sharp contrast to the cotton producers of the South, Northern wool producers were having absolutely no success in capturing the European market. Wool, just like cotton, was an indispensable raw material for textile production; the English, in particular, used great quantities of it. Even stranger, the English were increasingly dependent upon foreign sources for their wool; by 1850 not more than 40 percent of all wool consumed in England was raised on

England's own great sheep farms on the northern wolds. Between 1800 and 1850 England was importing thousands of tons of raw wool every year. These imports came, initially, from the great merino flocks of Spain. By 1850 German fleeces from Saxony and Silesia had entirely eclipsed the produce of Spain; England's average annual import of this German wool, in the decade of 1840-50, averaged about twenty-five thousand tons every year. This was the hard fact that puzzled John Brown: If Americans could grow wool every bit as fine as the people of Silesia and Saxony, and if they could clean their wool properly as he had instructed them, why should they not capture as big a share of the English market?

John Brown was perfectly right in believing that such a thing was possible, and that, if the option of exporting wool was open to the growers, it would exert pressure upon American wool buyers to pay the producers fair, competitive prices. But Brown's timing was poor. Perkins and Brown was a small business with a tiny staff; there was only John Brown himself, with the help of John Jr. and a couple of local wool sorters, to do all the work. Brown had neither the time nor the facilities to gather the vital information that he needed to make correct decisions about selling wool on the international market. 1849 was the worst possible year that he could have chosen for such an operation. There was, that year, an unprecedented glut of fine wool in Europe. English imports of German and Australian wool reached a high of thirty-three thousand tons, or eight thousand tons more than the average yearly imports for the decade of 1840-49. The English market could not absorb this surplus, and prices collapsed. So low did English prices fall that by the end of the year English buyers could buy this wool, ship it to the United States and, even after paying transportation costs, sell it to American factories for less than American growers were asking.

Brown's mission to sell fine American wools overseas was doomed even before he set sail from Boston on August 15, 1849. In England he sold all the wool entrusted to him by the growers at disaster prices, thereby losing forty thousand dollars, an enormous sum in those days. Brown and Perkins were ruined. His own superfine wool—"beautiful little compact Saxon fleeces, as nice as possible"—was sold at a loss along with the rest.

Musgrave, a Northampton, Massachusetts, manufacturer, had offered Brown sixty cents per pound for this wool three months earlier but Brown had refused to sell because the price was too low, and had shipped his wool to England. Musgrave now purchased this very same wool in London, and had it returned to him in the United States. He paid this time a price of fifty-two cents per pound, and this included the cost of transportation of the shipment across the Atlantic. The businessman, gloating over his triumph, invited "Uncle John," as he called him, to visit the warehouse and to inspect "the fine shipment of wool" that he had just received from England. As Musgrave's son tells it, "One glance at the bags was enough. Uncle John wheeled, and I can see him now as he put back to the lofts, his brown coat-tails floating behind him, and the nervous strides fairly devouring the way."

Beyond that, Brown's trip did little to boost the reputation of American fine wools in Europe. With so small a staff he was unable to give a thorough examination to every fleece he exported; and the result was predictable. On his return from England Brown wrote to Frederick Kinsman, a Northampton wool dealer, and told what happened:

> During the examination of some wool that was offered at . . . sale, search was made inside the fleeces. Unwashed wool and various kinds of filth and waste matter was found concealed in them. . . . Nothing will enable American wools to compete successfully in the British market but the opening and removing from every fleece whatever may be the least degree objectionable.

American wool producers, as Brown predicted, paid dearly for their failure to organize the industry on a competitive basis. The woolgrowers of New South Wales, in Australia, not the Americans, captured the British market for fine wools.

Returning to New York City at the end of October 1849, Brown spent a couple of weeks at North Elba, then went back to Springfield and started winding up the Perkins and Brown business. He was in his fiftieth year. His enterprise had not, as he fondly hoped, provided a "perfectly safe" way of making money; it confronted him with a failure as complete and as humiliating as his Ohio land speculations some fourteen years before.

7

"MY FAMILY IS POOR"
Last Years on the Western Reserve, 1851–55

> "Oh My Lord, wherewith shall I
> save Israel? Behold, my family is
> poor in Manasseh, and I am the least
> in my father's house."
> —Gideon, The Book of Judges

When John Brown returned to the United States in October 1849 he would have liked nothing better than to turn his back upon the failure of his wool business and to retire to the quiet of his Elba home. But he could see no way to disentangle himself quickly. He spent most of 1850 visiting wool producers in Pennsylvania, Ohio, and West Virginia, explaining to them what had happened and asking them to refund the money that Perkins and Brown had advanced to them in excess of the sum for which their wool was sold. There were stormy encounters. "I am meeting with a good deal of trouble from those to whom we have over-advanced," Brown wrote to John Jr.

Throughout 1850, while John Brown was on his travels, a crisis was unfolding in the nation's political life. In this year, Congress faced a decision that it could no longer postpone concerning the future of lands that the country had seized from Mexico in the war of 1846–48. The richest of these lands was the Mexican province of California, where gold was discovered in January 1848. This triggered a gold rush to the far West. People went by boat, a twelve-thousand-mile trip down the South American coast, around Cape Horn to San Francisco. They went by mule across the swamps of Panama. They went overland on the California Trail from St. Joseph, Missouri, two thousand heartbreaking miles through grasslands, mountains, and deserts. All over America, all over the world, men downed their tools, quit their farms, and set off to California to get rich. At the start of 1848 the white population of California was a bare 5,000; by early 1850 it had exploded to eighty thousand. These new Californians were hammering at the Union's door, seeking admission as a state.

The California pioneers were all free people; they wanted their new state to bar slavery. Many Northern congressmen supported this position, for throughout the North more and more voters were demanding that slavery be barred from all new states admitted to the Union. Southerners bitterly opposed this view. Senator John C. Calhoun, the slaveholding South's most eminent spokesman, opposed it more bitterly than any. Old and dying, he delivered his final speech to the Senate on a bright spring day, March 4, 1850.

Calhoun gave frank and ominous advice to the South. The population of the North, he pointed out, had been growing so fast that it far outstripped the population of the South, and this situation was destined to become rapidly worse. As a result, Southerners were now in a minority both in the Congress and in the country. If, said he, this Northern majority were friendly to the South, if it were neutral on the question of slavery, there would be no problem. But such was not the case; Northerners, on the contrary, were fiercely hostile to the interests of the slaveholders. These people, he warned, and the nation's Congress, which they would soon control, would start by barring the advance of slavery into all lands won by purchase or war. They would end by abolishing slavery throughout the South itself. "What is to stop this agitation," Calhoun asked, "before the great and final object at which it aims—the abolition of slavery in the South—is consummated? Is it, then not certain, that if something is not now done to arrest it, the South will be forced to choose between abolition and secession?"

Leave, Calhoun told his fellow Southerners; secede. If the Union tried to stop them, the blood would be upon its hands, not upon theirs.

The implication of this advice was clear enough. If the North challenged the South's right to secede, the South would fight; the two sides would come to blows over control of the North American continent.

Calhoun's view of the widening chasm between North and South and the bluntness of his words shocked Washington. Moderates on both sides hastened to work out an agreement—the Compromise of 1850—which, they hoped, would promise peace. The North received California as a free state, and the abolition of the slave trade in the District of Columbia. The South, in return for these concessions, got a Fugitive Slave Act with teeth.

For many years slaves had been running away by the thousands to freedom in Canada. Until about 1840 the recovery of runaways was not too much of a problem for the owners. A slaveholder went after his property or hired a slave hunter. Blacks were tracked down, manacled, and dragged back into slavery. But as antislavery feelings began to grow, these man and woman hunts aroused the fury of Northerners. Many free states passed laws to protect free black people from kidnapping, and also to provide a fair trial for persons accused of being fugitives. Thus it became ever more difficult and more expensive for slaveholders to catch runaways. By 1850 antislavery sentiment throughout the North had become so intense that in many places retrieving fugitives was a practical impossibility. Slavecatchers might expect violence at the hands of local people; some feared for their lives.

The Fugitive Slave Law of 1850 changed all this. Until then catching runaways had been the job of the slaveholder himself, with whatever help he might get from local police authorities in making arrests, issuing permits for removal, or holding slaves in jail until he was ready to transport them. Now the law of 1850 charged the federal government itself with the duty of catching slaves, and gave it the power to do so. The law appointed special judges (called commissioners) to supervise the return of runaways; federal marshals, as slavecatchers, were empowered to call upon *any* citizen who happened to be around to help them chase and arrest fugitives. Refusal to obey such a command became a federal crime. Commissioners, too, were entitled to employ "so many persons as they may deem necessary" to guard captured fugitives from people trying to free them, and to guarantee the return of such fugitives to the South. Federal troops were now at the disposal of slaveholders to protect them from antislavery action. The cost of all this protection, of course, was to be borne by the taxpayer.

The law of 1850 produced terror in Northern black communities. All people living there, free or slave, were now menaced by a new offensive of slavecatchers and kidnappers. Northerners began to seethe with rage at the spectacle of the federal government as a tool in the hands of tyrants to deprive human beings of their inalienable right to life, liberty, and the pursuit of happiness.

The Fugitive Slave Law of 1850 went into effect in the month of September; it was the month when Ruth Brown married Henry Thompson, a young Adirondack farmer whose family owned several farms in the region. In November Brown spent three happy weeks at Elba before going back to Springfield to wind up the affairs of the Perkins and Brown office there. He had reached the firm but reluctant decision to move back to the Western Reserve and to resume sheepherding as Perkins' partner. "Never before" he wrote to John Jr. after returning to Springfield early in December, "did the country [Elba] seem to hold out so many things to entice me to stay on its soil." But it was not to be. Perkins and Brown faced a blizzard of lawsuits from wool dealers and growers seeking damages; Brown could not honorably desert his partner until these suits had been settled. "Nothing but the sense of duty, obligation and propriety," as he told John Jr., "would keep me from laying my bones to rest at Elba; but I shall cheerfully endeavor to make that sense my guide; God always helping." The wisest place for him to have his base, he considered, was at Akron. There he would be in continual consultation with Simon Perkins. The boys—that is, Salmon, Watson and Oliver—would grow the crops, tend the sheep, and earn the family's living. Brown himself would make long, tedious trips to Boston, Troy, New York City, wherever it was necessary to go in order to prepare the cases and to defend the firm in court.

Back in the Springfield office after the fine visit to Elba, John Brown was homesick. "I feel lonely and restless," he wrote Mary, "no matter how neat and comfortable my room and bed, nor how richly loaded may be the table. . . ." He found escape from his worries by giving most of his free time

A Boston Meeting Protests the Fugitive Slave Act

Wendell Phillips, famous antislavery orator, addresses a meeting on Boston Common, April 1851, to protest the capture, under the Fugitive Slave Act of 1850, of Thomas Sims, a fugitive from Savannah, Georgia. The federal government returned Sims to Georgia under guard. There his owner had him publicly lashed with thirty-nine lashes as punishment.

—Gleason's Pictorial, *May 3, 1851*

to working with the Springfield black community and helping it to organize resistance to the Fugitive Slave Law. "I have improved my leisure hours," he told Mary early in 1851, "with colored people here, in advising them how to act, and in giving them all the encouragement in my power." Some of them, he went on, were so alarmed that "they cannot sleep on account of either themselves or their wives and children." He urged his own family to try and imagine that this nightmare was happening to *them*. Organizing work took up his time until far into the night. His effort on behalf of the black people, he said, "has prevented me from the gloomy homesick feeling which had before so much oppressed me. . . ."

In January 1851 Brown's work among the black people bore fruit with the formation of an antislavery organization called the League of Gileadites—from the story of Gideon, in the Book of Judges, who picked only three hundred men at Mount Gilead, the bravest of the brave, to smite the host of the Midianites.

For the meeting that brought this organization into being, Brown prepared some "Words of Advice," enjoining men and women alike to arm themselves with pistols, to resist the Fugitive Slave Law to their last gasp, and not to allow themselves to be taken alive. "Nothing," he told them, "so charms the American people as personal bravery, and the sight of one bold man defending his rights will arouse more sympathy than all the accumulated wrongs and miseries of a submissive colored population." Brown, too, had advice for his own family and his white friends. Join the runaways, he told them, in fighting any attempt to seize them, regardless of the punishment that may follow.

Forty-four black men signed the agreement that Brown presented to the meeting. "As citizens of the United States," the document said, "we will ever be true to the flag of our beloved country, always acting under it." John Brown believed the black people, whether slave or free, were American citizens and that, when fighting to defend their freedom, they were fighting for, and under, the American flag. And this was true, even if the fight for freedom obliged them to fight the troops of the federal government itself.

"We will provide ourselves at once," the agreement continued, "with suitable implements, and will aid those who do not possess the means, if any such are disposed to join us." The League of Gileadites was open to every colored person committed to black defense "whether male or female." The League was also open to the old and the young, who were charged with the specal duty of keeping guard and of giving "instant notice to all members in case of an attack upon any of our people." Officers of the League were to be chosen by the members not only for their wisdom but for their "undaunted courage."

John Brown did his work well. Three years later, long after he had left Springfield, the League of Gileadites still functioned, armed and vigilant, in the town. William Wells Brown, a fugitive slave who later became a famous writer, testified that slavecatchers knew well what the temper of the community was; they never dared molest fugitive slaves in Springfield.

In March 1851 John Brown left Springfield, picked up his family at North Elba, and headed for Akron. Ruth stayed behind to farm with Henry Thompson. "The family is on the road," he wrote to John Jr. and Jason on March 24, "the boys [Salmon, Watson, Oliver] are driving on the cattle, and my wife and little girls are . . . waiting for me to go on with them."

Jason and John Jr., who were managing the Akron farm in their father's absence, awaited his arrival with impatience. Both young men were now married and had purchased farms of their own in the Reserve. Their brothers, Owen, aged twenty-eight, and Frederick, aged twenty-two, needed help in running the big Perkins farm. Owen had been crippled since he was a child by an injury to his right arm; Frederick, whom his father described as "a very strong man," was the victim of chronic attacks of sickness during which he suffered from what were termed "wild spells." Brown himself denied that his son was insane. One of Frederick's uncles, Rev.

Samuel Adair, praised him warmly and wrote that he was "intelligent and judicious in spite of wild spells," and a "warm friend of the slave."

With John Jr. and Jason gone, and Brown himself frequently away, much of the farm work at Akron must have fallen upon the shoulders of Watson, aged sixteen, and Salmon, aged fifteen, with some help from Oliver, aged twelve. Watson and Salmon were fine, hardworking farmers and stockmen, hardy young adults fully capable of meeting all the responsibilities that were thrust upon them. As for Annie and Sarah, aged eight and five, respectively, they helped their mother in many ways in her work around the house and garden.

At Akron, the Browns continued to live in the same house that they had occupied before, opposite the Perkins mansion. There they remained for a full three years, until March 1854, when Brown and Perkins dissolved their partnership by mutual consent. By the end of this time John Brown no longer owned any share the the famous Perkins–Brown flock that he and his sons had built up with so much effort.

Perkins and Brown lost most of the suits brought against them by creditors, either in the lower courts or upon appeal; large sums were now added to the losses that the firm had to meet when it failed in 1849. Money had to be paid out in lawyers' fees, the travel expenses of Brown and his witnesses, and damages for the plaintiffs. Simon Perkins had to pay every penny of these debts himself. "I have no way," Brown wrote to his partner, "to share these losses with you." Brown's financial interest in the flock of sheep that he and Perkins owned together was now wiped out; the flock became Perkins' exclusive property as partial payment of all the money that Brown owed him.

In March 1854 the contract between Perkins and Brown came to an end, the lawsuits were over, and the two men parted company. Brown moved his family to a farm that he had rented from a man named Ward; there they stayed for more than a year. All that Brown had of his own in this world was a two hundred and forty-four acre farm at North Elba,

Mary Brown, with Annie and Sarah, 1851

This daguerrotype was probably made in the spring of 1852 after the family had left North Elba and returned to Akron, Ohio. Eight years later Annie, the sad-looking little girl on the left, would accompany her father to Harper's Ferry.

—*Library of Congress*

that he had bought from Gerrit Smith five years before, but had not yet paid for. He could not move back and live on this land, for he had no house there.

During the years of litigation, from 1851 to 1854, family life at Akron went on much as it had at North Elba. Whether he was on the road or at home, John Brown continued to write to Mary, to Ruth and Henry, to John Jr., and to Jason. To Mary he sent instructions about the care of the sheep and the conduct of the farm. The boys, he said, "should be with the sheep as constantly as possible, early and late." In good weather they should "take a good deal of pains to get to the best feed they can reach without having them exposed to severe storms—the lambs and old ewes in particular." In another letter he told his sons that after the spring planting "I would like them to repair the fences around the meadow and the upper corn fields. There are some rails in the woods below the pasture that may be gathered for that purpose." A letter written to Ruth and Henry from Akron announced the birth of a baby boy. "Our little one," he said, "has dark hair and eyes like Watson's." Six weeks later Brown wrote to John Jr. at his farm at Vernon that the child had died, and that he himself was sick with fever and unable to do much. He had words of praise for all his five sons, Frederick, Owen, Watson, Salmon and Oliver, who "have done remarkably well about the work."

A year after the Browns returned to Akron, in March 1852, Harriet Beecher Stowe published *Uncle Tom's Cabin*, the novel whose bold and passionate attack upon slavery thrilled millions of readers in the North and throughout the world. John Brown took the book with him on his travels, read it from cover to cover, and found words of high praise for it. "The star of hope," he wrote to Mary early in 1853, "is slowly and steadily rising above the horizon. As one sign of these times I would like to mention the publication of *Uncle Tom's Cabin* . . . which has come down upon the abodes of bondage like the morning sunlight unfolding…in a manner which has awakened a sympathy for the slave in hearts unused to feel.…" He was glad, he told Mary, that Annie and Sarah were helping their mother around the house, and he added: "I have bought for them *Uncle Tom's Cabin* to live in after I get home."

Late in 1853, as the time of the Brown family's stay at Akron drew to a close, a fresh crisis between North and South was about to erupt; like the crisis of 1850, it concerned the question of slavery in the West. By this time the tide of western settlement had spread as far as the middle reaches of the Mississippi River, and had spilled over into the broad valley on the other side. Two states that bordered the middle river on its western side had already been admitted to the Union—Missouri in 1821 and Iowa in 1846. The time had come to provide for the settlement of the huge region that lay directly beyond these states.

The crisis erupted when the South demanded that slavery be permitted to advance into this region, and the federal government gave its consent.

The territory to be organized was a major portion of the Louisiana Purchase that the United States received from France in 1803. This Purchase stretched from the Canadian border on the north to the Gulf of Mexico on the south, from the Mississippi River on the east to the Rocky Mountains on the west. Much of it was a realm of torrid summers and icy winters, a sea of waving grass where little rain fell and trees grew only along the watercourses. There the buffalo lived and roamed in countless numbers, and numerous tribes of Native American peoples followed and hunted them.

Back in 1819 a bitter quarrel erupted in Washington D.C. when Missouri applied for admission to the Union as a slave state. Northerners objected: Were the slaveholders, they asked, to be allowed to take their slaves anywhere in America? Where would it end? After much discussion among politicians from the two sections, Congress enacted an agreement known as the Missouri Compromise. Slavery would be allowed to advance only into the portions of the Purchase south of the parallel of latitude 36° 30'; the one exception was Missouri itself, which lay north of that line. Throughout the rest of the Purchase, and by far the bigger part of it, slavery was to be forever banned. (See map, page 90.)

Up until 1853, only one more state was admitted to the Union north of the 36° 30' line, and that was Iowa in 1846. Most of the rest of the huge expanse of grass, prairie, and timberland north of 36° 30' latitude was known as the Nebraska Terrritory. This was the territory west of Iowa and Missouri whose time had come, in 1853, for settlement. Law and government had to be set up so that settlers could move in, roads and railroads could be built, and Native American title to the land could be (as the phrase went) "extinguished."

At the end of 1853, Stephen Douglas took the lead in drawing up a bill that would accomplish this purpose. Douglas was a key figure in American politics: U.S. senator from Illinois, chairman of the Senate's Committee of Territories, and leader

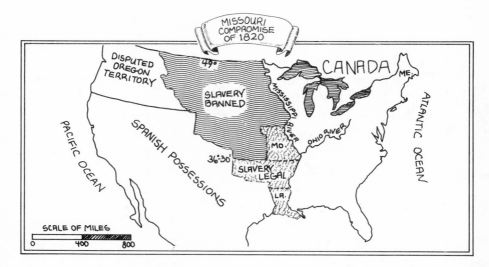

of the Democratic party. By that time railroads were starting to creep westward from the Mississippi across Iowa and Missouri. In just a few years they would reach Nebraska Territory, and land values were bound to rise where those railroads ran. Railroad shareholders and speculators who won title to this land, and then sold it off to the farmers coming in, were likely to make fortunes.

Stephen Douglas personally would have liked to promote the building of three transcontinental railroad lines—one in the North, one across the nation's midsection, and one in the South; but there wasn't enough money available for so ambitious a project, and Douglas had to choose a single route. A central track from Missouri westward seemed to have obvious advantages, but here Douglas faced opposition from the Southern members of his party. Southerners, with Missourians in the lead, were unhappy with this plan. It would, for one thing, result in the creation of a free state west of Missouri; this would make it easier for slaves to flee and would increase the insecurity of slave property in Missouri. A central railroad, for another, would in general speed up the formation of free states in the west and encourage the increase of a free, as opposed to slave, population. As Calhoun had warned in 1850, this would be the worst possible thing for the South.

Having said this, the Southern politicians came up with a proposal of their own. Certainly, they said, they would not be against the building of a central railroad through Nebraska Territory, but under one condition: the bill providing for the organization of the Territory must throw aside the old ban on slavery there, and must make the holding of slaves legal.

Douglas went along with this idea, and became, indeed, its most vigorous champion. The bill that he submitted to the Senate early in 1854, and that passed both houses of Congress in May, is known to history as the Kansas-Nebraska Act. This act split the Nebraska Terrritory into two parts—the more southerly, which was now called Kansas Territory, and the remainder, which continued to go under the old name, Nebraska Territory. (See map below.) Setting aside Nebraska and leaving it to be dealt with in the future, the act zeroed in upon the organization of Kansas Territory. Congress was given the authority to appoint officials for the territory, like a governor and judges. The old Missouri Compromise was repealed. The act did not go so far as to say that slavery was now legal in Kansas; it provided that the settlers themselves should decide, before the state was admitted to the Union, whether they wished to make slavery lawful or not. "Let the people decide by popular vote," said the act, "whether they

will admit slavery or not." "People," of course, meant "white settlers only."

The Kansas Territory that was thus organized stretched all the way from the Missouri border westward to the Rocky Mountains. Much of it was composed of the rolling grasslands of the high plains; but the eastern portion was well-timbered, well watered, and fertile. Broad rivers flowed through bottom lands that needed, as one traveler wrote, "nothing but the plough to convert them into fruitful fields." Beyond these river valleys lay the prairie, "the beautiful, undulating prairie, here and there a grove of walnut, hickory, oak or sugar maple, but for the most part a broad and treeless pasturage, stretching its velvety surface of grass as far as the horizon." In spring the grasslands were enameled with flowers of every hue; brilliantly colored butterflies fluttered through the air.

Passage of the Kansas-Nebraska Act produced a tempest of opposition in the North, but Senator Douglas controlled enough votes to secure passage of his bill by slim majorities. Southerners at once began to organize to ensure that the first settlers should be from the South, that they should beat Northern pioneers to the gun and make certain that the State of Kansas which they were setting up would be controlled by pro- and not antislavery interests. Societies called Blue Lodges were brought into being all over Missouri in order to launch a movement for the immediate settlement of eastern Kansas lands. Similar societies, too, were organized in other Southern states. During the summer and fall of 1854 proslavery settlers flowed into eastern Kansas. Free-state settlers also trickled in; one of their settlements, a cluster of log huts on the southern bank of the Kansas River, they named Lawrence.

By November 1854 the various settlements had been organized into nineteen electoral districts, and elections were held for a delegate to Congress. The Blue Lodges of Missouri rounded up their supporters, who marched across the Missouri-Kansas border, and cast many illegal votes for the proslavery candidate. They drove free-state voters away from the polls, and silenced or removed election officials who protested the fraud. An even more ambitious excursion was organized in March 1855, when elections took place for members of the first territorial legislature. This time the invading force was much larger. An army of close to five thousand Missourians arrived, organized in separate companies with marching bands, drums, banners, wagons, horses, and tents. Uttering blood-curdling oaths and swearing death to "abolitionists," these people spread through the election districts to cast their votes, many of them going through the polls not once but many times. As before, they beat up or chased away antislavery voters, and thus they procured the virtually complete victory of proslavery candidates.

When it was all over the Missourians reformed their columns, raised their flags painted with skull and crossbones, and retraced their steps to Missouri. These men, who thus ominously introduced a reign of terror into Kansas, were proud to call themselves "Border Ruffians." They were a rough-looking bunch, "hair uncut and uncombed," as one traveler described them, with "unshaven faces and unwashed hands." The handles of long-bladed Bowie knives stuck out from the tops of their boots; revolvers and swords dangled from their belts.

Not all Southerners in Kansas were like the violent, trigger-happy Ruffians. By the end of 1854 there were several hundred Southerners in the territory who had come to stay: to settle upon the land, to raise families and crops.

Pleasant Doyle, a farmer from Tennessee, was one of the people from the South who came to settle in Kansas. He and his wife Mahala had a large family, six boys, ranging in age from nine to nineteen, and a little girl. In October 1855 the Doyles packed their children and farm equipment onto two covered wagons and set out for Kansas driving their animals before them. They arrived early in November 1855, staked out a hundred-acre claim, and built themselves a cabin where they could pass the winter. The little settlement where the Doyles lived lay upon the northern side of Pottawatomie

Creek, not very far from where this stream flowed into the Osage River. When the Doyles arrived in Kansas they found that they were near neighbors of John Brown's sons, who had come to the Territory earlier in the year and settled a little to the north.

8

TO THE WEST
John Brown and His Sons in Kansas, 1854-56

> To the West, to the West,
> To the land of the free,
> Where the winding Missouri
> Runs down to the sea;
> Where a man is a man
> If he's willing to toil,
> And the Humblest may gather
> The fruits of the soil.
>
> —Folk Song

While the slaveholders moved to seize control of Kansas Territory, people in the free states were not idle. Companies sprang up to promote emigration to Kansas—to provide information about routes to take and places to settle, to raise funds for publicity, and to equip free-state settlers with that formidable new weapon, the breech-loading rifle. Pamphleteers and journalists painted a glowing picture of a western land flowing with milk and honey. Lecturers from Kansas toured the North, urging people to come and settle. This propaganda was effective; it helped to swell a stream of emigrants, some of whom came from New England and the mid-Atlantic states, but most from the Midwest. The stream started in the late summer of 1854 as a mere trickle; within a year it had turned into a flood.

John Brown's sons were among the first to catch "Kansas fever." In the early fall of 1854, when the excitement about the

Kansas-Nebraska Act was at its height, a lecturer from Lawrence made a stop at Akron. The visitor, as Salmon Brown recalled years later, praised the country, telling with enthusiasm of its fine soil and glorious climate. He invited his listeners to "settle in Kansas and help defeat the South in its effort to make that Territory a slave State."

This appeal excited John Brown's sons; it spoke both to their own self-interest and to their antislavery convictions. During the early fifties the young men were either living at Akron, taking care of Simon Perkins' sheep, or working tiny farms of their own. Life at the time was particularly hard for country people in Ohio. It was a time of drought, especially in 1854, when the sun blazed down for days on end from a cloudless sky, when the land was parched and the crops withered and died.

Listening to the news about Kansas, John Brown's sons were fired with a vision of life in a land where the blessed rain fell, where the earth was fertile, boundless, and, above all, cheap. "Uncle Adair," as Salmon wrote, "had already moved to Osawatomie; and five of us sons decided to follow: to grow up in a new country and to fight if necessary for freedom."

"Uncle Adair" was The Reverend Samuel Adair, husband of John Brown's sister Florilla. In 1854 Rev. Adair staked out his claim at Osawatomie, a fertile spot where Pottawatomie Creek flowed into the Osage River. (See map, page 107.) John Brown's oldest sons—John Jr., Jason, Owen, Frederick, and Salmon—followed their uncle. Pooling what little property they had, they planned to settle close to Uncle Adair and to help each other clear their lands and build their cabins.

The sons urged their father and Mary to go to Kansas with them. In the fall of 1854 Brown was "hard pressed," as he wrote to his daughter Ruth, "to go with my family to Kansas." The suggestion was logical enough. Brown, in middle age, was a poor man; all he had in the world was title to an upland farm on thin soil in the Adirondacks. Like his sons, he had much to gain and little to lose by moving out west. But "Father," as John Jr. told it, "did not at first sympathize very much with our ideas." In fact he rejected them out of hand.

For four whole years, ever since 1851, only the need to fulfil an obligation to Simon Perkins had kept Brown from moving back to North Elba. By the fall of 1854 his work was done, his obligation to Perkins fulfilled. Now he eagerly awaited the coming of spring, when he would be able to sell his fine Devon herd at a good price, move the family to New York, fulfill his heart's desire to live a peaceful frontier life in the hills that he loved. "It was in that mountain region of the Adirondacks," John Jr. wrote,

> that he desired to make his permanent home. He had cherished the idea that his children, a number of them at least, would like also to settle there, be reared and educated where pure air and water, where the odor of balsam and pine, of birch, maple and hemlock and where clear rivulets and dashing brooks, foaming waterfalls and placid lakes should ever be a source of inspiration.

John Brown's unwillingness to give up a life in North Elba grew even deeper when Mary gave birth to her thirteenth and final child on September 25, 1854. They named the baby Ellen in memory of the daughter who had died at Springfield in 1849. Brown had no doubt that these three daughters, Annie, Sarah, and Ellen, ought to be raised in the wilderness, just as he had been. He knew that there was more to education than sitting at a desk, figuring sums, and reading books. He believed that the wilderness was the place where children might learn life's most important lessons: how to live as independent, self-reliant human beings, rejoicing in hardship, the simple life, and quiet.

John Brown wanted to stay in the East himself; and he also wanted his older children to stay there too. In June 1854, when John Jr. was sending him glowing reports about cheap and fertile western lands, Brown responded to his son by saying that "he still felt that Essex County [in the Adirondacks] was the best place of residence for the whole family." He still dreamed that those bleak uplands would become not only his own home, but the home of generations of Browns to come. Kansas, in his view, was a diversion from the main purpose of life as he saw it: to live simply and to engage in the struggle for human freedom. He feared, as John Brown Jr. recalled, "the debilitating influence of milder climates, of the comparatively easy methods by which treasures could be laid up on earth." He feared that his older sons would be diverted from the main purpose to which they had twenty years before pledged themselves in mutual help—that of aiding the slave "to throw off his yoke of bondage."

The plea that John Brown should emigrate to Kansas to help his sons to settle there raised other questions as well. Had he not promised Gerrit Smith that he would go to Elba in order to help the black people become self-reliant farmers? Was it any less important to help these ex-slaves than to help his own sons? Had not the time finally come to fulfill his own life's dream: to strike a blow at slavery through its heartland in the hills of the South?

John Brown was torn between the urgency of his sons' pleas for help and his own doubts. He wrote a number of letters to people, asking their advice, and he asked Ruth and Henry Thompson to consult the black people themselves. "As I have volunteered in their service," he said, "they have a right to vote."

Brown's sons did not wait for him to make up his mind. Before 1854 had come to an end, they began to leave Ohio and head west. In October 1854, just one month after Ellen's birth, Owen and Frederick left, driving before them a small herd of cattle; among the animals were several prize Devons, their father's parting gift. The two brothers took the overland trail from Chicago to Meredosia in southern Illinois, where they wintered at their uncle Edward Lusk's farm. There, in the spring of 1855, Salmon linked up with them. Together the three brothers ferried the Mississippi and then headed straight across Missouri to the Kansas border and Osawatomie.

John Jr. and Jason were the last of the five sons to depart from Ohio. Their party numbered seven in all: John Jr., his wife, Wealthy, and their one son, Johnny; Jason and his wife, Ellen, with their two little boys, Austin and Charles. The two families placed their wordly possessions on board a river

John Brown in 1854

A drawing of John Brown as he appeared in 1854, in the prime of life, and on the eve of his voyage to Kansas.

—*Library of Congress*

steamer at Rochester, Pennsylvania, about thirty miles above Pittsburgh. In the spring of 1855 the boat took them down the Ohio River to the Mississippi, then northwards to St. Louis. There they transferred to another steamboat, the *New Lucy*, that took them up the Missouri, almost due west across the state of Missouri to Kansas City, right at the Missouri–Kansas border. Kansas City, at that time, was better known under the name of Westport Landing: a place where river boats docked in order to put ashore passengers and freight. The "city" was a scattering of huts on the south side of the river, with a few more perched up on the surrounding hills.

The *New Lucy* was crowded with Southerners, many of them Border Ruffians. They mixed drinking and gambling with boasts that they would kill all the "damned Abolitionists," or run them clear out of Kansas Territory. The Ruffians were well armed with revolvers and Bowie knives; John Jr. and Jason watched them with growing alarm. "For the first time," John Jr. wrote, "there arose in our minds the query: must the fertile plains of Kansas, through a struggle at arms, be first secured to freedom before free men can sow and reap?" John Brown's sons, were that to be the case, were poorly prepared for such work. All the arms that the five men had between them, John Jr. said, were "two small squirrel rifles and one revolver."

Cholera broke out among the passengers aboard the *New Lucy* long before the boat docked at Westport Landing. Many fell sick, some died, and among these was Jason and Ellen's beloved Austin, aged four. The family went ashore at the village of Waverly, some sixty miles from their journey's end, and as John Jr. wrote, "buried him at night near that panic-stricken town, our lonely way illumined only by the lightning of a furious thunderstorm."

Daylight was almost gone when the brothers finished spading soil over the tiny grave. Then the rain came down in sheets. The mourners sought shelter at a house on a fine, broad street bordered by towering locust trees. The master of the house received them kindly, even though he knew that they might be bearers of the dreaded cholera, and took them to a dry storehouse where they passed the night. In the morning he sent one of his slaves out to them with coffee and bread. John Jr. long remembered this kindness to grief-stricken travelers. "Though I have forgotten our host's name," he wrote many years later, "I am sure it is recorded in the Book of Life."

By early May 1855 all five sons and their families had reached Osawatomie. They settled on a tract of land a little less than two miles west of Uncle Adair. The place was beautiful beyond belief; they named it Brownsville. Ellen, numb with homesickness and grief for Austin, would not be comforted; but to the other Browns it seemed as though their troubles were surely over. "The lovely prairies and wooded streams," John Jr. wrote, "seemed to us indeed a haven of rest." In their mind's eyes the young men saw "cattle increased to the hundreds, possibly thousands, fields of corn, orchards and vineyards." Pitching their tents they set to work with a will to make their vision of prosperity come true. They ploughed the land, planted crops, began to fence fields and gardens. They cut and stacked hay to supply the animals for the winter.

The Browns were just a few of the free-state settlers who arrived in Kansas in the spring of 1855. An endless stream of wagons, at the rate of about fifty a day, ferried the Mississippi and then took the trail westward to Westport. By the end of May the Kansas borderlands were dotted with settlements of mostly free-state people, staking out claims upon the broad lands that lay between the Kansas River in the north and Pottawatomie Creek in the south.

The supplies that the settlers needed had to come through Westport. This gave the Border Ruffians a chance to spread terror. They waylaid the people as they traveled the trails between Westport and Kansas Territory, seized their money, flour, cattle or horses, wounded or killed them with little fear of arrest or punishment. T.H. Gladstone, an English traveler, wrote in 1855 that "murder and cold-blooded assassination were of almost daily occurrence. . . . Murderers, if only they have murdered in behalf of slavery, have gone unpunished; whilst hundreds have been made to suffer for no other crime than the suspicion of entertaining Free-state sentiments." The purpose behind this terror was stated clearly by *Squatter Sovereignty*, a proslavery newspaper. "We are determined," wrote the editor, "to make Kansas a slave state; though our rivers should be covered with the blood of the victims, and the carcasses of the Abolitionists should be so numerous . . . as to breed disease and sickness, we will not be deterred from our purpose."

Stories of robbery and violence against innocent people filtered down to Osawatomie from the north; the Browns went about their labors with a sense of foreboding. The proslavery legislature was to assemble in July at Lecompton. The brothers knew well the kind of laws that it would pass; that it would then call in the dreaded Ruffian bands to enforce its will. "War of some magnitude," John Jr. concluded, "now appeared to us as inevitable."

May 20, 1855, John Jr. sat down and wrote his father a long letter. "Salmon, Frederick, and Owen," he told the old man, "say that they never was in a country that begun to please them as well. . . . I know of no country where a poor man endowed with a share of common sense and with health can get a start so easy. If we can succeed in making this a free state, a great work will be accomplished for mankind." Then John Jr. appealed for help. "The interest of despotism," he wrote, "has secured to its cause hundreds of thousands of the meanest and most desperate men, armed to the teeth with Revolvers, Bowie Knives, Rifles and Cannon, [but] the friends of freedom are not one fourth of them half armed." In this situation, he went on, the free-state people could offer no real resistance "whenever their dearest rights are invaded and trampled down . . . by the miscreants which Missouri has ready at a moment's call to pour in on them."

To cope with this situation John Jr. proposed that the antislavery people should take immediate steps to arm themselves and to organize militia companies. Somebody, he said, had to take the lead, and the Brown sons were ready to do so. They were "not only anxious to fully prepare, but thoroughly determined to fight. . . . " He appealed to John Brown to send them revolvers, a cannon, and knives.

★　　★　　★　　★　　★

Early that May 1855 John Brown made a trip to Illinois to sell his Devon herd, taking Oliver with him. Oliver planned to work on an Illinois farm during the summer before moving on to Kansas. Having sold the herd, John Brown returned to Akron, picked up his family, and headed east. With Mary,

Watson, Sarah, Annie, and Ellen he arrived at North Elba in mid-June. They all settled into the little frame house that Henry Thompson had built upon the John Brown farm. The house was unfinished; no clapboards on the outside nor plaster inside covered the bare planks to provide protection from winter's biting cold.

In a few days John Jr.'s letter arrived from Kansas, with its plea for help. John Brown read it and finally made up his mind about going out west. Mary and the family would remain at North Elba; Watson would stay with them to work the farm. He himself would leave for Osawatomie to take arms to his sons and to fight alongside them. Later John Jr. told about his father's decision. "He soon obtained arms," wrote John Jr., and he added, mirroring his surprise, "but instead of sending, he came on with them himself."

John Brown spent most of July at North Elba, preparing for his trip. Late that month he said goodbye to Mary and the little girls and, along with Henry Thompson, Ruth's husband, headed west. At Rock Island, Illinois, Oliver joined them; the three moved slowly through Iowa into Missouri, carrying a heavy load of arms and supplies in a covered wagon. It was early September 1855. "The roads are mostly very good," John wrote to Mary, "we fare very well on crackers, herring, boiled eggs, prairie chicken, tea, and sometimes a little milk." At Waverly, Missouri, they stopped to take up the body of Austin Brown. Early October they reached Kansas Territory and came at last to Brownsville.

★   ★   ★   ★   ★

The travelers were shocked at what they found. Winter was coming on, but the cabins remained unbuilt. Most everybody was sick with fever; men and women huddled in their tents and "shivered over little fires," as John wrote to Mary, "all exposed to the dreadful cutting winds." Fields and gardens were unfenced; cattle roamed and trampled crops that lay unharvested.

John Brown and Henry Thompson set to work. One by one the others joined in as they regained their strength. They

gathered in beans, pumpkins, and squash, and picked the wild
grapes and hickory nuts that grew in the bottomlands. These,
along with corn bread and a little milk, provided them with
their Thanksgiving fare. They began to raise a cabin for Jason
and Ellen, building a wooden chimney daubed with clay on
the outside that would hold a good fire. They set about building a second cabin for John Jr. and Wealthy, but freezing
weather set in before much progress could be made. So they
drove stakes into the ground on three sides of the half-built
structure and packed bundles of prairie grass in between the
stakes to give some protection against the merciless winds.
Out in front they piled a stack of logs. "This," wrote John Jr.,
"duly replenished, furnished abundant heat in days and nights
when for weeks the mercury ranged from zero to twenty
degrees below."

While the Browns were planting their lands and struggling
to survive upon their claims, the conflict in Kansas between
free and slave-state people was coming to a head. Early in July
the proslavery lawmakers, who had been elected as a result of
the interference of the Border Ruffians in the March elections,
met at Shawnee Mission, close by the Missouri border. They
passed a code of laws blotting out the right of people in the
territory to freedom of thought, speech, and press. People
convicted of uttering even a single word in opposition to
slavery could now be given a sentence of five years in chains,
laboring on the roads. People who helped slaves to flee, or
who had in their possession books that dealt with slave
resistance or rebellion "shall," in the words of section 3 of the
code, "be guilty of a felony and suffer death." As a journalist
commented at the time, "the man who possesses a copy of
Uncle Tom's Cabin is now on a par with a murderer."

The free-state settlers faced an illegal, oppressive government, to which they could look in vain either to protect their
physical safety or their freedom. Some of them, therefore,
began to organize a government of their own. On October
23—just after John Brown arrived in the territory with Oliver
and Henry—a free-state convention came together at Topeka,
a village on the Kansas River some seventeen miles west of

Lawrence. The delegates drafted a constitution under which a free-state government would be set up early in 1856.

When winter was over there would be two governments in the Kansas Territory claiming the obedience of its people. The proslavery leaders decided to crush this new free-state threat to their power. As Lawrence was the center of free-state resistance, the proslavery people targeted the town for destruction and summoned a new invasion of Border Ruffians to accomplish this purpose.

Lawrence, as Sara Robinson, a Holyoke Massachusetts emigrant described it, was "a little hamlet on the prairie, set in a land with sloping hills, rolling meadows, and timbered creeks." All around, the landscape was dotted with the cabins of free-state pioneers. A handful of New Englanders settled at Lawrence in 1854; the population grew rapidly in 1855, log huts gave way to buildings of brick and stone. The Border Ruffians made their first attack upon this "Abolitionist nest" in November 1855, but were obliged to retreat when free-state leaders persuaded the Lecompton governor, Wilson Shannon, to sign a truce. The episode inspired the Lawrence people to fortify their town. Throwing up earthworks they organized militia companies, and conducted daily drills and nightly patrols.

Winter, with winds whipping the snow and driving it like the desert sand, brought these struggles to a close for a little while. In March 1856, the free-state government assembled at Topeka, and the crisis flared with a new intensity. Franklin Pierce, president of the United States, immediately declared that the Topeka movement was an unlawful challenge to established authority. He authorized the Lecompton government to call in United States troops to seize the "rebel" leaders, and to put down the rebellion.

The president's message provided Lecompton's leaders with the green light for which they had been waiting. On Thursday, May 22, news reached Brownsville that Border Ruffians, assembled at Westport, were poised for an invasion of Lawrence. John Brown, Jr., was now both a member of the Topeka legislature and captain of his own militia company, the Liberty Guards. He galloped off to spread the news and to round up his men. They assembled at Theodore Weiner's store, and headed northward along the trail to Lawrence, twenty-five miles away. John Brown, his sons, and Henry Thompson accompanied the militiamen (see Map, page 107).

Four miles south of Theodore Weiner's store lay the tiny settlement of Shermanville, at a place where the trail crossed Pottawatomie Creek. A scattering of proslavery people lived at Shermanville: Henry Sherman, who kept a store by the trail and was the postmaster; Allen Wilkinson, a member of the proslavery Lecompton legislature; Pleasant and Mahala Doyle, settlers from Tennessee. Little love was lost between the Shermanville people and their neighbors at Brownsville, a few miles to the north. The Browns said out loud that the Lecompton government was a fraud, that they defied its laws, that all of Kansas and all of the United States ought to be rid of slaveholders and of slavery. The Browns hated and feared "Dutch Henry" Sherman and Pleasant Doyle because they were friends of the Border Ruffians; they provided Ruffians with hospitality during their raids into the territory, and they fingered leading free-state people as targets for the Ruffians to bully, rob, or kill. The Shermanville settlers, on their side, made no secret of the fact that they regarded the Browns as free-state ringleaders. The Browns, in their eyes, were indeed marked men, slated, one way or another, to be driven out of the territory.

Soon after midnight, in the early morning of May 23, the Liberty Guards, and John Brown with them, crossed the Osage River on the journey northward to Lawrence. Then a messenger arrived; he told the startled, angry militiamen that the Border Ruffians had taken Lawrence without a fight, and that they were leveling it to the ground with cannon fire. John Jr. was not certain what he should now do. He moved his men into camp a mile or two up the trail, to wait and see what would happen.

The Border Ruffian attack upon Lawrence and the failure of the Lawrence people to fight back threw John Brown into a fury. After breakfast that morning of May 23 he called

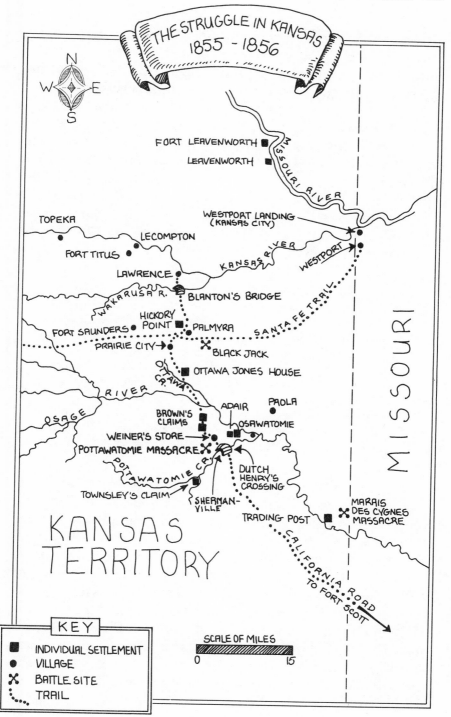

THE STRUGGLE IN KANSAS
1855 - 1856

N
W E
S

FORT LEAVENWORTH
LEAVENWORTH

MISSOURI RIVER

WESTPORT LANDING
(KANSAS CITY)

TOPEKA

LECOMPTON

FORT TITUS

KANSAS RIVER

WESTPORT

LAWRENCE

WAKARUSA R.

BLANTON'S BRIDGE

HICKORY POINT

PALMYRA

SANTA FE TRAIL

FORT SAUNDERS

PRAIRIE CITY

BLACK JACK

OTTAWA JONES HOUSE

OTTAWA CR.

RIVER

PAOLA

OSAGE

BROWN'S CLAIMS

ADAIR

OSAWATOMIE

WEINER'S STORE

POTTAWATOMIE MASSACRE

DUTCH HENRY'S CROSSING

POTTAWATOMIE CR.

TOWNSLEY'S CLAIM

SHERMAN-VILLE

TRADING POST

MARAIS DES CYGNES MASSACRE

M I S S O U R I

KANSAS
TERRITORY

CALIFORNIA ROAD
TO FORT SCOTT

KEY
■ INDIVIDUAL SETTLEMENT
● VILLAGE
✕ BATTLE SITE
•••• TRAIL

SCALE OF MILES
0   15

together a small group of men and held a council of war. It was time, he told them, to strike against the Ruffians and their friends in the territory, to show them that they could not terrorize and kill innocent people without having to pay a price. Some of the proslavery people, he said, must be killed in such a way, as he put it, "to cause a restraining fear."

Brown's little group included Theodore Weiner, the storekeeper; James Townsley, a Pottawatomie Creek settler; his four sons, Frederick, Owen, Salmon, and Oliver; and Henry Thompson. Soon they were to be seen sharpening a few swords that Brown had brought with him from the East, and packing supplies in Townsley's wagon. One of the militiamen remembered that an old man:

> ventured to ask Brown what movement was now on foot. He replied that he was going to regulate matters on the Pottawatomie. 'Well, Captain Brown,' said the old gentleman, 'I hope you will act with caution.' The Captain suspended his packing arrangements for a moment, looked the stranger in the eye, and said: 'Caution! Caution! These are always the words of cowardice.' From the firm and deliberate manner in which these words were spoken, no person ventured to question his course. All knew the determined spirit of the old Captain, and I think I may safely say that every one in camp expected to hear of some bold stroke at the proslavery ruffians.

John Brown's little group climbed into Townsley's wagon, then headed southward down the trail. Early that evening they reached the Pottawatomie at Shermanville, and went into camp between two steep, dark ravines. There they remained for twenty-four hours, until late in the evening of Saturday, May 24. Walking quietly in the dark of the night Brown and his men then attacked the Shermanville settlers. Banging on the Doyles' door they aroused the sleeping family. John Doyle, aged sixteen and the third of Pleasant Doyle's sons, told what happened. "They came into the house, handcuffed my father and two older brothers and started to take me, but my mother begged them to leave me as I would be all the protection she would have."

Brown allowed John Doyle to stay in the cabin; Pleasant and his two older sons were led away. "Haven't I told you what you were going to get for the course you have been taking?" Mahala Doyle screamed at her men. "Hush, mother," Pleasant Doyle replied.

Later that night John Doyle went out to look for his brothers and his father. He found them lying lifeless on the road or in the tall grass that grew nearby. All had been stabbed or hacked to death with swords. Allen Wilkinson and William Sherman, a brother of "Dutch Henry," shared the same fate. Neighbors found the bodies lying in the brush or at the edge of the creek, with gashes in the heads, breasts, or sides.

★   ★   ★   ★   ★

Even if we accept Brown's claim that free-state people needed to inspire a "restraining fear" in their enemies, the Pottawatomie murders were senseless. Armed struggle is a tragic and cruel thing, but there are ways to check and restrain an enemy without dragging unarmed men from their beds and butchering them in cold blood.

The massacre on Pottawatomie Creek was an indefensible act. It highlights the worst features of John Brown's character—his "commanding disposition," his indifference to the advice of others, his blind fury overriding the voice of reason and mercy. Lessons may be drawn from this that apply to our age as well as to his own. Vile acts may not be committed in pursuit of any ideal; they taint the person who commits them and they challenge the worthiness of his cause. Brown never admitted publicly that he bore the responsibility for this crime. Not until many years later did the truth become widely known. It would have destroyed the image that Brown presented in his last years as a freedom fighter. Oswald Garrison Villard, one of John Brown's most eminent biographers, sums it up. "For John Brown," he wrote,

> no pleas can be made that will enable him to escape coming before the bar of historical judgement. There his wealth of self-

sacrifice, and the nobility of his aims, do not avail to prevent a complete condemnation of his bloody crime at Pottawatomie. . . . If he deserves to live in history it is not because of his cruel, reprehensible acts on the Pottawatomie, but despite them.

9

ARMED STRUGGLE IN KANSAS
The Brown Family in the Field,
1856

The Border Ruffians' destruction of Lawrence in May of 1856 was a turning point in the struggle for the freedom of Kansas. Up until that time the Southern slaveholders had had matters pretty much their own way in the territory. They had rigged elections, dictated a constitution, and set up a puppet government that permitted free-state people to be plundered, terrorized, and assassinated. After the sack of Lawrence this situation began to change, for a new mood of opposition was growing up among the free staters. Their patience exhausted, they were starting to brush aside political leaders who counseled obedience to the illegal or "bogus" Lecompton government and its laws. After Lawrence, free-state men mounted their horses and took to the bush. Concealment was not difficult; creeks and streams that flowed across the prairie were often heavily timbered. At times they passed through deep ravines. Guerrilla bands could live in the neighborhood of these watercourses and move from place to place with little danger of discovery.

Lawrence spelled an escalation of violence in Kansas, and the coming of civil war. John Brown's vengeful act gave expression to the fear and smoldering fury among many free-state people that now, in a single terrible flash, reached the kindling point. Pottawatomie, as Reverend Samuel Adair wrote on May 23, was a sign that "the gun which the Border Ruffians have been firing has begun to kick."

Like other free-state people, John Brown took to the bush at the end of May. After Pottawatomie he was an outlaw with a price upon his head; federal troops and Border Ruffians alike scoured the countryside in search of him. His band was composed of Brown himself, his sons, with the exception of John Jr., his son-in-law, Henry, and a handful of other settlers from the Osawatomie region. Their first campsite was in the thickets of Ottawa Creek. John Brown took charge of the cooking. "We had two meals daily," said August Bondi, one of the band, "consisting of bread, baked in skillets, washed down with creek water mixed with a little ginger and a spoon of molasses to each pint." James Redpath, a St. Louis journalist who accidentally bumped into the campsite, has left a vivid description. "Near the edge of the creek," he wrote,

> a dozen horses were tied, all ready saddled for a ride for life, or a hunt after Southern invaders. A dozen rifles and sabres were stacked around the trees. In an open space, amid the shady and lofty woods, there was a great blazing fire with a pot on it; a woman, bareheaded, with an honest, sunburnt face, was picking blackberries from the bushes; three or four armed men were lying on red and blue blankets on the grass; and two fine-looking youths were standing, leaning on their arms, on guard near by.

As for John Brown himself, Redpath wrote, "he stood near the fire, with his shirt-sleeves rolled up, and a large piece of pork in his hand. He was cooking a pig. He was poorly clad, and his toes protruded from his boots."

John Brown and his men were now *guerrillas*—bush fighters, free to ride early or late, to sleep under the stars, to attack their enemy as they chose, to live by laws of their own, not the slaveholders', making. But John Brown's two oldest sons, John Jr. and Jason, had a different experience. Neither of these brothers had participated in the Pottawatomie raid but had remained with their militia company, the Pottawatomie Rifles, in the Prairie City area after John Brown left. Before the company dispersed and the men went back home, John Jr. with a few of his friends visited the home of a slaveholder near Palmyra. They seized the man's two slaves, a boy of fifteen and a girl of eighteen, took the young people back to camp, and liberated them. They told these slaves, Jason remembered, that "you belong to no human master, or mistress, but to yourselves, and you are free." This, of course, defied the Lecompton government and its brutal slavery code. Under this code John Jr. and his friends were liable, if caught, to be hanged.

The news of what John Jr. had done spread; the reaction among the militiamen was one of shock and anger. Bitter discussions broke out; the fate of the two young slaves, indeed, split the Pottawatomie Rifles down the middle. Liberation of the two, some of the men argued, would provoke retaliation: the slaveholder who had had his property taken away would tell the Lecompton authorities. Word would spread among the Border Ruffians that the Pottawatomie Rifles were a bunch of abolitionists, all of them. Innocent free-state settlers and their families would be exposed afresh to the danger of harsh punishment—the burning of homes and crops, homelessness, hunger, death. These free-state settlers, for sure, did not want slaves in Kansas; but they didn't want free black people there, either. They had little quarrel with slaveholders, or with their right to hold blacks as property, or with their proslavery views. All they asked of such people was that they stay in the South. Certainly, they said, these people might come to Kansas *to settle* if they wished, for that was their right. But they must not seek to seize unlawful control of the Territory, to rule it by force and terror, or to cross the border at will, with arms in their hands, and attack peaceable settlements.

Some of the riflemen took the two young slaves and returned them to their owner. Then the troopers disbanded and began to wind back down the trail to their homes. As they proceeded southward a man rode up on horseback with the news that "five proslavery men had been killed on the Pottawatomie Creek and horribly cut and mutilated, and that old John Brown and his party had done it."

Coming right after the crisis provoked by the liberation of the two slaves, this news was a shock to John Jr. and Jason. Both were sensitive and compassionate people. Jason could not bear the sight even of a trapped quail in its death agonies, much less the suffering of a human being. "The thought," he wrote later, "that my father and his company could do such a thing . . . nearly deprived me of my reason at the time." As for the riflemen, some of them began to boil with fury; the fear of retaliation now became very real.

News of the Pottawatomie killings was too much for John Jr., and he resigned his command. He and Jason understood very well that they were in danger. If the Border Ruffians caught them they might be tortured or killed in revenge for their father's act. Jason, indeed, fell into the hands of the Border Ruffians almost at once; they put a noose around his neck, flung the rope up over the limb of a tree; the intervention of a kindly judge from Kentucky saved his life at the last moment. John Jr. suffered a mental breakdown and fled to the bush. A few days later a band of Missourians found him in the timber near Osawatomie. Both brothers were taken as prisoners to Paola, the capital of Lykins County about seven miles from Osawatomie. Along with other prisoners they were placed in the hands of federal troops to be taken to Lecompton for "further examination."

The men endured a long, agonizing trip in the heat of the Kansas summer. Jason and the other prisoners were permitted to travel in a wagon; special treatment was reserved for John Jr., for he was a member of the free-state Topeka legislature scheduled to meet at Topeka the next July 4. Henry Pate, a Border Ruffian who had been deputized as a U.S. Marshall, headed the squad that inflicted punishment. "I was driven," John Jr. said later, "on foot at the head of a column a distance of nine miles at full trot to Osawatomie. My arms were tied behind me . . . so tightly as to check the circulation of blood, especially in the right arm, causing the rope, which remained on us twenty-seven hours, to sink into the flesh." John's feet, too, were bloody and gashed by the flinty beds of the streams through which he was forced to run.

At Osawatomie the prisoners were chained together by twos and driven westward along the wagon road. Florilla Adair, John Brown's sister, stood at the door of her cabin, a few yards north of the trail, and watched them pass. To the prisoners she gave a little food, to their federal guards she gave a tongue lashing. "What does this mean in this land of the Free," she raged, "that you drive these men like cattle and slaves?"

As the brothers plodded northward along the California Road under their guard, John Brown hid with his band in the thickets nearby, watching and waiting for the chance of a rescue. Reports would reach the guards once in a while, that John Brown had been seen. Captain Woods, in charge of the detachment, would send his men out to search. "The men would spend themselves," Jason recalled, "hunting along the river bottoms, through dense, prickly tangles, and come back at night worn out and furious, their horses done." There was, in actuality, little chance for John Brown to free his sons. He knew they were not only prisoners, but hostages. As Woods told Jason, "if such a rescue be attempted, and you try to escape, you will be the first ones that we will shoot."

John Jr. remained a prisoner, mostly at Fort Leavenworth, for nearly three months, until the middle of September 1856. The scars of his Kansas experience remained with him for the rest of his life. When he died, forty years later, his children found the marks of those terrible Kansas wounds still upon his body. Jason was let go before John Jr., in June. He went back to Brownsville to find the cabins laid in ashes, the fields desolate and abandoned. Wealthy, Ellen, and the children had fled to Osawatomie and taken refuge with the Adairs. All traces of the settlement the Browns had worked so hard to build were fast being covered by grass and weeds.

Captain Henry Pate, having assisted in rounding up John Jr. and Jason, stayed on in Kansas Territory in order to continue the search for John Brown himself. At the end of May he and his Border Ruffian band went into camp at Black Jack, a place near the Sante Fe trail five miles to the east of Prairie City, where a spring of fresh water gushed up amid a stand of tall dark oak trees. It was there that John Brown and his men, joined by another band under Samuel T. Shore of Prairie City, attacked their hunters in early June. Brown wanted to drive the intruders from the Territory and also to capture prisoners whom he might exchange for John Jr. and Jason.

Brown and his party surprised Henry Pate at dawn on June 2. After a fight lasting two hours Pate and 24 men surrendered to Brown's force. Pate was surprised and upset to find that he had given up to a mere handful of free-state men. But Brown lost his valuable prisoners when a group of U.S. cavalrymen under Colonel Edwin Sumner, commander of Fort Leavenworth, rode into his camp. Col. Sumner, interestingly enough, compelled Brown to free his prisoners but did not arrest him. He knew that such an act would not bring peace to the territory but would only intensify the anger of free-state people.

Black Jack was significant as the first victory of free-state fighters in open battle with a proslavery band. Brown's name now became a symbol for all free-state people in Kansas in the struggle to rid the Territory of the Missouri invaders. Among Border Ruffians he won the reputation of being a fearsome enemy.

Sometime in June Jason found his way back to his father's band and joined it. A welcome letter arrived from Mary about the middle of the month. Watson, wrote Mary,

> has sowed about four acres of Rye and is agoing to sow some Carrots and turnips & plant some potatoes & occupy all of the land there is cleared off. Watson is not idle I can tell you. It is a cold raw day & the snow is not all gone in the fields yet & plenty of it is to be seen on the mountains. The beech and maple trees look almost as dry as they did in January hardly a bud is to be seen on them yet."

John had sent Mary some money, and she was thankful for this. "What we have now received" she wrote, "will pay up all of our debts and some over to get leather for shoes. The girls and I have not had any since we came here & I have made all Ellen has had this winter out of cloth." Ellen, Brown's youngest daughter, was, at that time, two years of age.

"We have," John Brown wrote back, "like David of old, had our dwelling with the serpents of the rocks and wild beasts of the wilderness, being obliged to hide away from our enemies . . . nearly destitute of food, clothing, and money." Henry and Salmon had been badly wounded at Black Jack; the others suffered from recurring episodes of malarial fever. Free-state friends and neighbors on Ottawa Creek—especially the Ottawa Indian, Jones, and his New England wife—helped nurse the men.

Early in July John Brown visited Lawrence. He went to see William Phillips, the correspondent of the *New York Tribune*, and invited him to accompany Brown and his men on a trip to Topeka. The free-state assembly, which had been set up by the constitution of 1856, was scheduled to meet there on July 4. Both the Lecompton proslavery authorities and the administration in Washington had made no secret of the fact that they would not tolerate the existence of this challenge to the established proslavery power in Kansas. It was inevitable that they would break the gathering up. John Brown hoped that the legislators would resist anybody who dared to try and disperse them, including the troops of the United States itself. He wanted to be on hand to see what would happen, and to take part in the struggle.

Phillips was glad to go along; he too wanted to observe and report the confrontation between the free-state people and their proslavery antagonists. That night, on the way to Topeka, they camped upon the open prairie, under the stars. Brown and Phillips placed their two saddles together as pillows, and Brown spread his blanket upon the wet grass. Both men lay down upon it, with Phillips' blanket to cover them. Throughout the night they talked—or rather Brown did, and Phillips listened.

"In his ordinary moods," the journalist wrote, "the man seemed so rigid, stern, and unimpressible when I first knew him, that I never thought a poetic and impulsive nature lay behind that cold exterior. The whispering of the wind on the prairie was full of voices to him, and the stars as they shone in the firmament of God seemed to inspire him. 'How admirable is the symmetry of the heavens,' he said, 'how grand and beautiful!'"

Brown talked, among other things, about the need for fundamental reforms in American life. Society, he considered, was organized upon far too selfish a basis; men and women followed their lives thinking only of themselves and their own personal interests; this diminished their stature as human beings. He lamented the fact that "there was an infinite number of wrongs to right before society would be what it should be;" but he stressed that, for his generation, the top priority must be given to the struggle to do away with slavery. "Slavery," he said, was "the sum of all villainies and its abolition was the first essential work." The American people must grapple with slavery and bring it to an end. If they did not, "human freedom and human liberty would soon be empty names in these United States."

On July 4 Col. Sumner marched into the room where the free-state legislators had assembled, and said, "Gentlemen, this is the most disagreeable duty of my whole life. . . . You must disperse." Sumner had five companies of soldiers in the street outside to enforce his command. The assemblymen left meekly without making any fuss.

With the free-state government destroyed, most of Brown's sons decided to leave Kansas. By July 1856 they and their families were disillusioned with life in the territory. Their dreams of happiness had vanished into a nightmare. Their homes were in ashes, their precious cattle stolen or strayed. They had had their fill of icy winters and flyblown summers, of fevers, fighting, and bloodshed.

Even worse, they had seen a frightening buildup of the proslavery forces, backed by the federal government itself. While the Browns were living and fighting in the bush in the spring and early summer of 1856, the Missourians were build-ing a line of forts in eastern Kansas. They used these forts, or wooden blockhouses, to stockpile guns, ammunition, and supplies of food at key points. Forts appeared at New Georgia, on Middle Creek eight miles up the Osage River from Osawatomie; at Franklin, four miles southeast of Lawrence; at Fort Titus, just south of Lecompton; and at Fort Saunders, on Washington Creek about half way between the Kansas and Osage rivers. From these and other strongholds, wrote Judge James Hanway, a highly esteemed Pottawatomie settler, the Border Ruffians would "sally forth, steal horses and cattle, in-tercept the mails, rob stores and dwellings, plunder travelers, burn houses and destroy crops." Their aim was to terrorize the free-state people and to drive them out.

The campaign of terror did drive many settlers out, but it also made others determined to stand and fight. John Brown was one of those. Frederick decided to stay with his father. Jason and Ellen, along with Charles, would stay until John Jr. could be freed from jail. Wealthy, John Jr.'s wife, also stayed with their child.

When news reached John Jr. that four of his brothers were preparing to leave Kansas, his feelings were mingled joy and relief. At the end of the month he wrote from Leavenworth to his father, telling him how glad he was about his brothers' decision. "Where I shall go if I get through this is more than I can tell," he wrote, "of one thing I feel sure now, and that is that I shall leave Kansas. I must get away from exciting scenes to some secluded region, or my life will be a failure. . . ."

At the beginning of August John Brown and Frederick escorted the departing men to the Nebraska border in an old covered wagon hauled by a brace of oxen. Owen, Salmon, Oliver, and Henry lay inside, sick with fever. John Brown and Frederick plodded along on foot. A band of free-state volunteers, going by on the trail, recognized the old man, and cheered. "In passing I looked at him closely," one of them remembered. "He was rather tall and lean, with a tanned, weather-beaten aspect. He looked like a rough, hard-working farmer. . . . His face was shaven, and he wore a cotton shirt, partly covered with a vest. His hat was well worn, and his general appearance, dilapidated, dusty, and soiled. He turned from his ox team and glanced at our party from time to time as we were passing him. No doubt it was a pleasing sight for him to see men in armed opposition to the Slave Power."

Having seen his sons across the Nebraska line and safely out of reach of the Border Ruffians, John Brown turned back. There were political as well as personal reasons for his decision to stay. Not only was John Jr. in prison; it was also clear by the end of the first week in August that the struggle was increasing in intensity and was, in fact, coming to a head.

The systematic terror practiced by the Border Ruffians was a two-edged sword. As Judge Hanway put it, "these frequent inroads of the Ruffians into the Territory produced *a retaliating spirit* on the part of the free-state men," whose numbers were growing. Before August some of the bands which the free-staters formed to avenge the raids actually crossed the border into Missouri and destroyed the homes of people who had participated in Border Ruffian attacks. In August the free-state fighters took the offensive in Kansas as well, targeting the forts which were key parts of the Missouri occupation plan. Free-state bands attacked and demolished the Border Ruffian strongholds one after the other. New Georgia came first, on August 5; Franklin was razed on the 14th; Fort Saunders the next day; Fort Titus the day after that. Blockhouses went up in flames, large supplies of guns, ammunition, and food were seized or destroyed. Border Ruffians fought, fled, and died.

In the face of this situation the Border Ruffians made a last all-out effort to save their dying cause. The leaders of this final offensive were David R. Atchison and John W. Reid. Both men were generals in the Missouri state militia, but Atchison was, in addition, one of the state's most powerful politicians. As a high-ranking member of the Democratic party and a U.S. senator, he was a close ally of Stephen Douglas in steering the Kansas-Nebraska Act through Congress. Atchison was a powerfully built, red-faced man "six foot two inches tall and as straight as an arrow." Here was a man, twelve years a

U.S. Senator, resorting to naked force to plant slavery in Kansas in defiance not only of the will of its settlers but of the Constitution itself.

The two generals mobilized a force of close to two thousand men. Appeals to Missourians to rally to the cause were made in the border counties. "Let every man who can possibly leave home," said one circular, "go now to save the lives of our friends. . . . Let no one stay away. We need the old men to advise, the young to execute."

Thus appealed to Missourians assembled at the end of August at the tiny border town of New Santa Fe. Atchison and Reid planned a two-pronged offensive aimed at Osawatomie in the south and Lawrence and other free-state centers in the north. A member of the invading party gave a clear statement of the objective of the invasion, which was launched on August 29. "*We expect*" he wrote, "*to clear the whole Territory of Abolitionists before our return.*"

John Brown and Jason arrived at Osawatomie a few days before the attackers. Brown's plan was to fight in the area south of Osawatomie, driving Border Ruffians back across the border and warning proslavery settlers of the peril they faced if they continued to work with the Missourians in bringing war to Kansas Territory. On August 29 messengers arrived from Lawrence, among them Frederick. They brought urgent pleas from free-state people in the north to come to the defence of Lawrence, which, they believed, Atchison would attack at any moment. Brown decided to camp that night on the heights above the Osage River, north of Osawatomie. In the morning he and other free-state groups in the area would move north to help in the defense of Lawrence.

At dawn on the morning of August 30 General Reid struck—at Osawatomie. During the night he circled round to the south, crossed Pottawatomie Creek, and moved in from the west. As the sun rose he and his men came down the wagon road, heading toward the town. A local proslavery settler named Martin White rode ahead of the main party, which numbered two hundred and fifty men. White had a cabin near the Osage River, a few miles upstream from Osawatomie.

Frederick Brown was the first person to meet the raiders, a mile west of town. He had risen early to take care of the horses that had been stabled overnight at his Aunt Florilla Adair's home, close to the trail. White reined in his horse and cried "Halt!" Frederick came toward him, unarmed. "I know you!" he said. Martin White's answer was a rifle bullet shot through Frederick's heart.

Rev. Samuel Adair hurried out of his cabin and found Frderick lying dead in the path. He dashed back and warned his family. Charles Adair, aged twelve, leaped on his pony and galloped into town to arouse the people. Then he crossed the Osage and sped up the hill on the other side, where Brown and his men were camped. "We were just getting our breakfast," one of Brown's men recalled, "when we saw the little fellow coming up the hill on his pony under the whip. Brown recognized his nephew . . . and stepped out to meet him. Charlie shouted, 'The Border Ruffians are coming and have killed cousin Frederick.' John Brown simply said, 'Men, come on, we must meet them before they get to town.'"

The free-state force, numbering no more than thirty-five men, made no effort to defend Osawatomie. John Brown ordered most of the men to take cover among the trees that fringed the Osage River northwest of town, where the stream ran parallel to the trail and a few hundred yards to the north. From this sheltered position they rained bullets on the Ruffians advancing along both sides of the trail in a skirmish line. Reid's men began to fall; others dismounted and advanced toward the timber on foot. The free-state men drew back to the river in good order and then waded across. One man was killed and three or four others were taken prisoner. The Missourians dared not pursue Brown and his men. They proceeded instead to Osawatomie, plundering and firing houses, driving off cattle. John Brown watched from the other side of the river, as smoke spiraled up from the settlement. Tears rolled down his cheeks. "God sees it," he said to Jason.

Reid's men, rather than press on with their plan to sweep the territory of "abolitionists," straggled back to Missouri. So did Atchison's men, who also burned and plundered in the north but did not dare attack Lawrence. The invasion accomplished little beyond turning more free-state settlers into homeless refugees. But Osawatomie marked a turning point in the struggle for Kansas. The determined opposition of a tiny group of men had checked a far larger force of Border Ruffians.

In September, 1856, Kansas became the focus of national attention. It was the central issue in the presidential election campaign. A new political party, the Republican, emerged with a single plank in its platform: *Stop the bloody struggle in Kansas; stop the spread of slavery in the territories.* The administration of Franklin Pierce, thus prodded, bestirred itself; it appointed John W. Geary as governor of Kansas Territory. Geary was a tough, forthright Pennsylvanian who knew exactly what he wanted to do. Arriving in Kansas on September 9, 1856, Geary decided that he would disband all unlawful fighting forces. This was bad news for the Border Ruffians. It meant that there would be an end to armed proslavery intervention in Kansas.

Governor Geary was true to his word. Senator Atchison lunged at Lawrence on September 17 with an army Geary estimated at 3,300. The governor confronted this force at the head of U.S. troops and ordered it to disband. Reluctantly, Atchison marched his men back to Missouri.

At the same time that Governor Geary arrived in Kansas John Jr. was released from his Leavenworth jail. With his son free and the fighting apparently over, Brown got a welcome breathing spell. He could return east to see his family, to grieve with them for Frederick, to recover from the fever that had plagued him—and to raise funds to continue the struggle.

Early in October John Brown left Kansas with John Jr. and Jason and headed north along the trail to Nebraska. Ellen, Wealthy, and the children headed home by the less arduous Missouri River route. The old man was stretched out in the wagon, suffering from dysentery and fever. "When we left," he wrote Mary on October 11, "there seemed to be a little calm for the present in Kansas; cannot say how long it will last." He told his wife that he intended to return to the territory "if the troubles continue and my health will admit."

Though it did not become clear for several months, the proslavery forces had, in point of fact, lost their battle for control of Kansas. In the spring of 1857 a new horde of free-state settlers poured into the territory, coming by the Missouri River route. Dismayed Border Ruffians stood in the streets of Westport and watched the throng passing by. "My God!" Judge Hanway heard one say, "The cause is lost." "I'll be damned if it don't look like it," said another.

10

A FREE BLACK STATE FOR THE SOUTH
The Chatham Constitution
1857–1858

By December 1856 John Brown, with John Jr. and Jason, was back in the East. He had fully recovered from the fever, and a single idea was now in his mind—to raise the funds, guns, and equipment that he needed for a force of volunteers with which to operate in Kansas. Under the impression that the peace in Kansas was only a temporary lull, he wished to prepare for a renewed struggle. The thought was in his mind that he should seek to overthrow the proslavery government of Missouri itself; for the state of Missouri provided the base from which the slaveholders were making their attacks upon Kansas. As he put it when talking to William A. Phillips late that year, "It was only fair, as Missouri had undertaken to make a slave state of Kansas, . . . that Kansas should make a free state of Missouri."

As a base for his own operations John Brown selected the Quaker community of Tabor, Iowa, which lay twenty miles north of the Kansas line. Here, even before departing for the East, Brown had begun to store guns and supplies at the home of the Rev. John Todd. Early in 1857 Brown visited Boston and called upon the secretary of the Massachusetts State Kansas Committee; his name was Franklin Sanborn, a Harvard graduate who taught school at Concord. The young man was instantly drawn to the sunburned warrior from the Kansas plains; he found in John Brown a hero whom he could adore. Sanborn offered to help Brown "to raise and arm a company of men for the future protection of Kansas." Sanborn also introduced his friend to a number of wealthy, influential Bostonians; an informal John Brown support committee soon emerged. This group—later to be called the "Secret Six"—helped raise funds, first for a volunteer force in Kansas, and then for the assault upon Harper's Ferry. Besides Gerrit Smith and Franklin Sanborn its members were George L. Stearns, a wealthy Boston businessman; Thomas Wentworth Higginson, the antislavery pastor of the Worcester Free Church; Dr. Samuel G. Howe, a pioneer in the treatment of deaf and blind people; and the Rev. Theodore Parker, the most famous and learned New England preacher of his generation.

John Brown spent most of his time, during the early months of 1857, touring New England and New York in order to talk about Kansas and to raise money, guns, and equipment for his volunteer project. "I am trying," he told audiences, "to raise from twenty to twenty-five thousand dollars in the free states, to enable me to continue my efforts in the cause of freedom. Will you afford me some support in this undertaking?"

John Brown was quite successful in raising funds and getting gifts of guns and supplies while he was in the East, but he did not get as much support as he hoped he would. The timing of his appeal was none too good. Kansas was now at peace and no longer on the front pages of the daily papers; public interest had subsided. Brown was discouraged by what he took to be peoples' indifference to slavery and the continued menace that it presented to the republic. Just before returning to Kansas he wrote, speaking of himself, that he was leaving

> with a feeling of deepest sadness; that after having exhausted his own small means, and, with his family and brave men, suffered hunger, cold, nakedness, and some of them sickness, wounds, imprisonment in irons; with extreme cruel treatment, and others, death; . . . destitute of shelter and hunted like wolves . . . he cannot secure even the necessary supplies of the common soldier.

The antislavery cause, he ended by pointing out, was one in which *"every man, woman, and child of the entire human family has a deep and awful interest."*

Yet John Brown did not go back to Kansas empty-handed. The Massachusetts State Kansas Committee made over to him more than two hundred breech-loading rifles, which had already been sent out to Kansas and stored with the Rev. John Todd at Tabor, together with thousands of rounds of ammunition. Then there was the matter of the pikes. When John Brown took Henry Clay Pate prisoner at Black Jack, he captured with him a number of pikes—wicked-looking weapons with doubled-edged blades attached to the end of long poles. In Collinsville, Connecticut, a blacksmith named Charles Blair attended one of Brown's lectures; Brown discussed with him the manufacture of hundreds of these weapons for shipment to Kansas. In the hands of settlers, he thought, they might come in very useful for defense against Border Ruffian attack.

So John Brown and Charles Blair signed a contract in March 1857. Blair produced 1,000 pikes, but not in time for them to be used in Kansas; they became part of the heavy load of weapons that Brown took with him later to Harper's Ferry.

All in all, it is estimated that, both in cash and supplies, Brown raised more than twenty thousand dollars, at that time a considerable sum. A small part of these funds he used to hire a military instructor, whom he planned to send out to Tabor to train the volunteers. This was an English soldier of fortune named Hugh Forbes, whom Brown met on one of his visits to New York City, where Forbes was scratching out a living as a fencing instructor and literary hack.

During this visit to the East in 1857 Brown tried to provide for his family, in case he lost his life in the Kansas struggle which he saw ahead. Mary and the three children, Ellen, Sarah, and Annie, were living on land that did not belong to them, for John Brown still owed Gerrit Smith a large sum of money on the purchase of his North Elba farm. Brown, accordingly, appealed to his Massachusetts friends to help him liquidate the debt. "For one thousand dollars," he wrote to

Amos A. Lawrence, wealthy Boston cotton manufacturer, "I am offered an improved piece of land which with a little improvement I now have made, might enable my family . . . to procure a subsistence should I never return to them." The family, he added, had "gone through the two past winters in our open cold house, unfinished outside, and not plastered. I have no other income or means for their support."

Several people agreed to subscribe to this project; later in the year Franklin Sanborn gathered the money together and made the payment for the farm to Gerrit Smith. Linked, too, with ownership of the farm was John Brown's concern to preserve his own memory and good name in the event of his death. That April while on a visit to Canton, Connecticut, he found in the graveyard there a large granite stone that had been set up in memory of Captain John Brown who died in the revolution "almost to the day," as John Brown wrote to John Jr., "eighty years from the death of his great grandson, Frederick Brown, in Kansas."

Brown made arrangements to have his grandfather's gravestone moved to North Elba. "I value the old relic," he wrote, "much the more for its age and homeliness; and it is of sufficient size to contain more brief inscriptions." Frederick's name was the first of the new "inscriptions" to be added to the stone. From his grandfather to his son Brown saw his family's sacrifice as part of a single, continuing struggle. He realized well that soon there might be other names that would need to be chiseled into the granite. "If I should never return," he wrote to Mary as he headed back to Kansas later that spring, "it is my particular request that no other monument be used to keep me in remembrance than the same plain one that records the death of my grandfather and son. . . ."

Three more names would be inscribed upon the old stone in 1859; John, Watson, and Oliver. Visitors to North Elba farm at Lake Placid, New York, may see them there to this day.

Fund raising and personal arrangements finished, John Brown visited the family at North Elba at the end of April to say goodbye. "The parting with my wife and young children," he wrote to Sanborn, "lay heavy upon my heart.

They were without income, supplies of clothing, provisions, or even a comfortable house to live in or money to provide any such things."

This time, on the trip to the West, Owen was the only one of his sons to go with John Brown. The journey was slow and tedious; but to Brown's satisfaction the rifles sent forward by the Massachusetts Kansas Committee were awaiting him at Tabor. He checked them out; most of them were in good order.

For three long months, from August until the beginning of November 1857, John Brown remained at Tabor—idle. This delay in getting into motion in Kansas infuriated Brown's backers, especially Thomas Wentworth Higginson. They had given him money only so that he could go and fight in Kansas; what then, they asked, was he doing?

John Brown spent weeks in Iowa waiting for news of fresh Border Ruffian raids into Kansas, fresh battles in which he might be called upon to participate. He dawdled away his time and no news came. Slowly it dawned upon Brown that the situation had changed: The slaveholders had lost their bid to control the territory and the free-state people had won. The worst was over. Kansas was no longer the main theater of antislavery struggle. This conclusion was confirmed by the results of the October 1857 elections for the territorial legislature. Free-state candidates won thirty-three of the fifty-two seats in the legislature—a clear majority. The elections were held in peace and the Border Ruffians made no effort to interfere. This was a far cry indeed from the elections of 1855 and 1856!

John Brown's conclusion was an important one. It meant that he was free to leave Kansas. The time had come, at long last, to carry out the plan that he had presented to Frederick Douglass some years back: to invade the land of slavery itself. Thus it was that he finally visited Kansas in November 1857 to recruit a fighting force for use in Virginia.

John Brown assembled his volunteers at Tabor. The group included John E. Cook, Aaron Stevens, John H. Kagi, C.P. Tidd, and William H. Leeman, all of whom went with the old man to Harper's Ferry. When they had assembled, Brown told the men that they would pass the winter training in Ohio and that their ultimate destination was Virginia.

The news came as a shock to some of the recruits, who assumed that they were preparing for continued action in Kansas. After a sharp dispute they all agreed to go east with Brown. Picking up the supplies that had been collected at Tabor, they hauled them all the way back across Iowa to Springdale, the railroad depot at the eastern edge of the state. This was the first step on the road to Harper's Ferry. "At Tabor," as John Cook testified, later, "we procured teams for the transportation of about two hundred Sharpe's rifles, which had been brought on as far as Tabor the year before, awaiting the order of Captain Brown. There were also other stores, consisting of blankets, clothing, boots, ammunition, and about two hundred revolvers . . . "

This equipment, originally destined for Kansas, was of critical importance for John Brown's Harper's Ferry campaign. In the months that followed, these supplies would all be shipped from Springdale to Chambersburg, Pennsylvania, which Brown was to use as a base for the Harper's Ferry operation. There was no thought in Brown's mind of going to Harper's Ferry to seize weapons. On the contrary: He took with him to Harper's Ferry most of the equipment, *including weapons*, that he needed, first, to seize the Armory, and, second, to establish a military base in the hills.

Most of December 1857 was spent hauling the heavy load two hundred miles clear across Iowa. Once the party arrived in Springdale, Brown left his men there for training under Hugh Forbes, who had been summoned from New York City. Brown himself hurried on to the East, arriving at Frederick Douglass' home in Rochester, New York, at the end of January 1858. He wrote to Mary and the family to tell them of his safe return. "Whether I shall visit you this winter or spring," he said, "I cannot now say; but it is some relief of mind to feel that I am again so near you. . . . The anxiety I feel to see my wife and children once more I an unable to describe."

In seclusion at Rochester, Brown began to write a constitution which he now believed was essential for the success of his Virginia plan. The Kansas experience had brought about changes in his thinking. The original Springfield plan had focused on destroying slavery by making slave property insecure, as slaves fled either to the mountains or northward to Canada. But now it seemed to Brown that this liberation process was far too slow. His revised plan, accordingly, called for the rapid creation of a free interracial state in the heart of the slave South. Such a state could be a powerful force, he believed, to disrupt the slave empire from within.

An invasion of the South, certainly, might start with the creation of a series of outposts, or armed forts, in the Appalachian Mountains—just as Brown had imagined would happen in the earlier plan. But, in order to destroy slavery swiftly, it must go far beyond that. The territory seized would have to be enlarged with time, until it could reach slaves not only in Virginia and the upper South but the deep South too. This zone, furthermore, must not merely be an area where scattered bands of guerrilla fighters operated; no, it must be created as a community of citizen-soldiers exercising political as well as military power. A new free state would organize and defend itself not only with the help of guns but also with the power of law to unify its people, to define their goals, and to lead their struggle.

During three weeks with Douglass, Brown threw himself into the task of drawing up the system of law on which the new state would stand. "When he was not writing letters," Douglass recalled, "he was writing and revising a constitution. . . . His whole time and thought were given to this subject. It was the first thing in the morning, and the last at night. . . ."

John Brown's "Provisional Constitution for the People of the United States" was drawn up in the name of the oppressed citizens of the country. He defined "oppressed citizens" as those who, "by a recent decision of the Supreme Court are declared to have no rights which the white man is bound to respect." Here he was referring to the Dred Scott decision of

1857, in which the Court ruled that the black people of the United States, whether slave or free, were not and could never be American citizens.

The provisional constitution set up a government with a president, a single-chamber assembly, and a court system whose judges would be elected, as would the president and the members of the assembly. A commander in chief of the citizen soldiers was to be appointed by a majority vote of the president, assemblymen, and judges.

Clause 28 of the constitution dealt with property. The members of the new Southern free state were to be toilers as well as fighters; they were to cultivate the soil and pursue their crafts for the benefit of all. Everything produced by the labor of the citizens, the clause said, was to be held as the property of the community, and to be used for the common benefit. This was in accordance with the early Christian ideal that believers should share everything in common. Shared by many Americans in the early years of the republic, this ideal found expression in a number of experiments in communitarian living that dotted the United States in John Brown's time.

Brown, as might be expected, had no scruples about seizing the property of slaveholders. Clause 38 of the constitution provided that the property of slaveholders, or those who fought against the new state, "shall be confiscated and taken, whenever and wherever it may be found, in either free or slave States."

In setting up his constitution and preparing to organize armed resistance, Brown was taking the law into his own hands. Like other revolutionaries before him, he believed not only in the righteousness of his cause but in the need to use armed force in order to win freedom. If he failed in this effort, he well realized that he might be hanged as a traitor. The danger did not move him. History, he believed, would judge in the end whether he was right or wrong.

When the draft of the provisional constitution was complete Brown invited the Committee of Six to meet with him at Gerrit Smith's estate, to discuss it. Only Franklin Sanborn and Gerrit Smith were able to attend. There, at Peterboro, New

York, on a long winter evening at the end of February 1858, John Brown unfolded the plan of his Virginia campaign—"to the astonishment and almost dismay of those present," as Sanborn wrote. Brown told his listeners that he had made his arrangements, that he had supplies, weapons, and men. He proposed May of that year for the attack and asked the committee for support and additional funds.

The discussions went on for two days; Brown's supporters were fascinated by the audacity of his plan but they had serious doubts that so colossal an undertaking could be accomplished by so few, and with so little. Gerrit Smith finally made up his mind that the committee ought to support the old man. "You see how it is," he said, "he has made up his mind to this course and cannot be turned from it. We cannot give him up to die alone: we must support him." A few days later Brown went to Boston, informed the other members of the committee of his plans, told them about the discussions in Peterboro, and won their endorsement.

The committee's doubts were understandable. Even if Brown were successful in establishing a base in the hills—and that was a big "if"—the Southern states would not tolerate armed abolitionists on their territory. They would mobilize their own troops against Brown and his men; they would summon the federal government itself to come to their aid. An overwhelming military force would descend upon the outlaws from all sides.

The committee members pressed this argument on Brown. But he was immovable. He was God's instrument, carrying out His divine purpose. "If God is with us," he said to his friends, "who can be against us?"

John Brown was a stubborn and persuasive person. He conveyed a feeling of utter confidence in himself and his plans. Franklin Sanborn explained why he prevailed with the Committee.

> We saw this lonely and obscure old man choosing poverty before wealth, renouncing the ties of affection, throwing away his ease, his reputation, and his life for the sake of a despised race and for zeal in the defense of his country's ancient liberties.

Moved by his example, shamed by the generosity of his soul, was it natural, asked Sanborn, that young men who thought themselves devoted to the antislavery cause would hold back upon the grounds of mere prudence? "Without accepting Brown's plans as reasonable," he wrote, "we were prepared to second them merely because they were his."

The next step for Brown was to submit his provisional constitution to the black community and to win the support of black leaders. He chose the town of Chatham, Canada, as the site of a secret constitutional convention. Chatham was a thriving port on the Thames River, a few miles upstream from Lake St. Clair. It was a haven for American fugitives who fled to freedom along the underground railroad from Detroit on the west side of the lake.

The convention opened in the second week of May, after a month of intensive efforts by Brown to have black leaders from the United States attend. The thirty-six blacks who came to the convention were mostly Canadians, but among them was a famous abolitionist leader from Pittsburgh, Martin R. Delany. Brown's volunteers, who had passed the winter in Springdale, were also there. He made a special trip back to Iowa in mid-April to fetch them east.

The Chatham meetings were in a one-room hut: the enginehouse of Fire Company Number Three, organized by the black people of the town. Brown opened the meeting by reporting in a general way on the plan to invade Virginia and establish a fighting force in the Appalachian Mountains. "He pictured himself with his faithful band," one listener reported, "safe in an impregnable mountain fastness, directing and leading to victory over the militia of the States and the Army of the United States, the free Negroes of the North and the countless slaves that would immediately rise all over the South and flock to his standard."

Brown's address expressed a deep faith that it was possible to win. It was equally clear that the risk of failure or death did not daunt him. "He intended," as one participant wrote,

> to sacrifice himself and his followers for the purpose of arousing the people of the North from the stupor they were under on

this subject of slavery. He seemed to think a few white men had to be sacrificed to awaken the people from a deep sleep that had settled upon the minds of the free whites of the North. He knew well that the sacrifice of any number of Negroes would have no effect.

Then Brown presented the provisional constitution to the assembly for approval. It was adopted without discussion, with one exception. Article 46 stated that the constitution must not be interpreted in any way "to encourage the overthrow of any State government of the United States; and looks to no dissolution of the Union. . . . And our flag shall be the same that our Fathers fought under in the Revolution."

On this question there was a lively exchange of opinions among the participants. Some thought that it would be madness to attack Virginia while the United States was at peace; better to wait until the country was at war with "some first-class Power;" then the chance for victory would be greater. Brown was outraged by this suggestion which he considered "a great insult." He was no traitor, he said, and would be the last man to take advantage of his country in the face of a foreign enemy. He insisted that the struggle against slavery was a national struggle—a struggle of the American nation itself against its most deadly foe. This was a struggle not for the dissolution of the Union but for its salvation; it would carry on the great battle for freedom which Brown's own grandfather and other revolutionaries had initiated in the American Revolution itself. The American flag, he said, belongs to us, the people, not to the slaveholders.

J. Monroe Jones, a Chatham printer, listened with great interest. To him, John Brown "appeared intensely American; he never for a moment thought of fighting the United States as such, but simply the defenders of human slavery in the States. Only the ulcer, slavery, was to be cut from the body politic."

The convention over, Brown and his men were preparing to depart when he was summoned to Boston by an urgent letter from the Committee of Six. Hugh Forbes was in Washington, D.C., it said, telling congressmen about the invasion plans.

11

SOUND AN ALARM
Why John Brown Went to Harper's Ferry, 1858–1859

> Blow ye the trumpet in Zion,
> and sound an alarm in my holy
> mountain . . .
>
> —The Book of Joel

The Committee of Six moved rapidly when they received news that Hugh Forbes was in Washington and that he was talking about the projected invasion of Virginia. John Brown was planning his attack with weapons that, as far as the public knew, were the property of the Massachusetts State Kansas Committee. The public had paid for them under the impression that they were to be used for the defense of Kansas. If this diversion of the committee's property were to become known, leading members of the committee, like Sanborn and Stearns, would face, to say the least, a public storm. The Secret Six, therefore, instructed Brown that the rifles must not be used, except in Kansas. They informed him that he must go back to Kansas immediately and carry on his operations there until the Kansas Committee had made it clear to everybody that it no longer had ownership or control of the weapons. This delay was also necessary in order to find out how much damage Forbes had done as a result of his Washington visit. As it turned out, Forbes' trip to the capital had little effect. People whom he talked to did not believe his story and dismissed him as a tiresome crank.

John Brown accepted the Secret Six's decision reluctantly; he could do nothing at all without their support. Back he went to the West, but without any specific instructions. The Secret Six, indeed, preferred to be left in the dark about his plans. Gerrit Smith spoke for them all when he wrote to Sanborn that "I do not wish to know Captain Brown's plans; I hope he will keep them to himself."

John Brown was back in Lawrence by the end of June 1858. Kansas Territory as a whole was quiet, though troubles continued in two counties, Linn and Bourbon, bordering upon Missouri. Free-state settlers were in a majority there, but Border Ruffians were still making raids, burning cabins, and driving off cattle. Disorders had reached their peak just a few weeks before John Brown returned. On May 19 Charles Hamilton, a Border Ruffian who came from Georgia, invaded a peaceful settlement not three miles west of the Missouri line in Linn County, and north of a settlement on the Osage River called Trading Post. (See Map, page 107.)

It was a fine spring morning; the free-state settlers were out in the fields, busy planting their crops. It was still early in the day when Captain Hamilton came up the wagon trail from the south with a band of thirty-two Ruffians. They crossed the ford at Trading Post and began to collect prisoners from among the people in the fields. Then they drove their victims in front of them like cattle.

Brought to the place of execution, some of the victims turned and glanced quickly behind them. They saw a green valley; years of toil had turned it from a wilderness of brush into a flowering land. They were lined up in a nearby ravine and shot down. Of eleven men, five were killed. Only one escaped uninjured. Soon two women arrived to find their husbands dead. They put the wounded onto a wagon and brought them back down the trail to Trading Post. One of these survivors was Elias Snyder, a blacksmith.

Early in July John Brown, using the name of Shubel Morgan, arrived in Linn County with a handful of volunteers and moved onto Snyder's farm. He had come to do what he could to defend the area from further attacks. "Deserted farms and dwellings," he wrote Mary, "lie in all directions for some miles along the line, and the remaining inhabitants watch every appearance of persons moving about with anxious vigilance. . . . A constant fear of new troubles seems to prevail on both sides of the line."

Here Brown and his men waited for several weeks, but nothing happened. The Swan Lake (*Marais des Cygnes*) massacre, as it was called, marked, as a matter of fact, the last of the Border Ruffian forays into Kansas. Even while John Brown waited on the farm, Kansas settlers were flocking to the polls to vote in a referendum in which they rejected the proslavery Lecompton constitution by an overwhelming eleven thousand votes out of a total of thirteen thousand cast. Finally, the struggle for Kansas was at an end.

During the month of August John Brown, stricken with fever, lay ill at his sister Florilla Adair's cabin at Osawatomie. On recovering he made several trips to Lawrence to raise money; on one of these he asked the *Tribune* correspondent, William Phillips, to meet with him. This was the last of three interviews that Phillips had with Brown, and the most important. Brown now made public the reasons why he felt that slavery must be overthrown by force and why the slaves themselves, as soldiers, must play a central part in accomplishing that task.

William Phillips published his report after the Civil War had ended. It is a document that shows John Brown as a person with a keen grasp of the realities of slavery in America.

Brown began by telling Phillips that the Constitution of the United States was an antislavery document: "the whole spirit and genius of the American Constitution," he said, "contemplated the early overthrow of slavery." Abraham Lincoln himself would echo Brown's thesis and elaborate upon it in a speech which he delivered less than eighteen months later at the Cooper Institute in New York City, and which launched his effort to secure the Republican party nomination as candidate for president of the United States. "As the Founding Fathers marked it," Lincoln would say, "so let it again be marked, as an evil not to be extended. . . ."

Antislavery sentiment, Brown continued, remained dominant in the American republic for its first twenty-five years—until, that is, the conclusion of the War of 1812. At that time slave-grown produce, and notably cotton, rapidly became profitable: "the desire grew to extend and increase it." As this happened, the condition of the black people grew steadily worse, "and the despotic necessities of a more cruel system constantly pressed on the degraded slaves."

Brown then dealt with the next big step that the slaveholders took to help them control the nation and to guide its destiny. "The pecuniary interests," said he, "that rested on slavery seized the power of the Government. Public opinion opposed to slavery was placed under a ban." Here Brown was putting his finger upon a fact of American life that few people as yet understood. The most powerful slaveholders had, step by step, won control of the federal government itself. In the United States Senate, due to the incessant formation of new slave states, slavery interests stood on an equal footing with those of the North. In the House of Representatives the South enjoyed political power far in excess of what it was really entitled to even though it had fewer representatives than the North. This was due to the Three-Fifths Compromise of the federal Constitution, which permitted the slave states to count three-fifths of their black population in determining the number of representatives which they might have.

As for the presidency, slavery interests had, since the time of Andrew Jackson, been able to secure the election of a number of presidents who could be relied upon to advance their cause—James K. Polk, Zachary Taylor (himself a slaveowner), Franklin Pierce, and James Buchanan.

Most dramatic of all was the South's domination of the United States Supreme Court. By 1858 five out of the nine members of the Court were Southerners, including Chief Justice Roger Taney, the son of a Maryland slaveholder. These were the men who, the previous year, had handed down the decision in the *Dred Scott* case. This ruling declared that black Americans had no rights that the people of the United States needed to respect, or that the federal government needed to enforce. Slaveholders, said the Court, could not be barred from taking their slaves into any territories—including Kansas—where the American flag flew.

John Brown drew certain conclusions from his analysis. Americans took up arms in 1776 to rid their country of British tyranny. The overthrow of British rule solved a problem that threatened American survival. Only a few years later, Americans were faced by the rise of yet another tyranny, as dangerous and as cruel as the first; slavery was moving to blot out the experiment in democracy which the American people had launched at the cost of so much effort and the shedding of so much blood. Had the slave masters seized Kansas they would have won a victory that "would have been the death-knell of republicanism in America."

The free-state victory in Kansas, Brown went on, was a severe blow to the slavemasters' plans to retain control of the federal government. "They are checked," said he, "but not beaten. They never intend to relinquish the machinery of government into the hands of the opponents of slavery. It has taken them more than half a century to get it, and they know its significance too well to give it up." In 1860 there was to be a presidential election. What, Brown asked, would happen if the Republican party elected its candidate? He gave his answer to this question in one word: war.

The Republicans, said Brown, had only a single issue on their political platform: *leave slavery alone in the South, but put an end to its expansion into United States territories.* If a Republican president were to be elected, said he, the game was up for the slaveholders. They would not be able to control the U.S. government any more; they would therefore quit the Union. "The moment they are unable to control," he said, "they will go out, and as a rival nation alongside, they will get the countenance and aid of the European nations, until American republicanism and freedom are overthrown." Once again the American people would have to take up arms and battle for their freedom.

Phillips called Brown's remarks "prophetic." The South followed precisely the course of action that Brown predicted, thus bringing the American Union to within a hair's breadth of destruction. At the time, to Phillips, what Brown said "simply appeared as incredible, the dream of a man who had allowed one idea to carry him away. I told him he was surely mistaken. . . ." Peace, said Phillips, had come to Kansas, and the fighting was over.

"No," Brown answered, "no, the war is not over. It is a treacherous lull before the storm. *We are on the eve of one of the greatest wars in history*, and I fear slavery will triumph, and there will be an end of all aspirations for human freedom."

Phillips thought that Brown was referring to continued border warfare in Kansas. He observed that such a thing was futile. Changing the subject, John Brown began to talk about the role of the black people in the coming struggle and of his desire to lead them. He cited the example of Spartacus, who led the slaves of ancient Rome in a revolt that shook the Roman Republic to its foundations.

Phillips observed that the Roman slaves were not the same as the American ones. "I reminded him," said the journalist, "that Spartacus and Roman slaves were warlike people in the country from which they were taken, and were trained in arms in the arena. . . . The Negroes were a peaceful, domestic, inoffensive race."

"You have not studied them right," said Brown, "and you have not studied them long enough. Human nature is the same everywhere." In a comment that gave just a hint of his own plans, Brown told Phillips that Spartacus might have overthrown Rome had he "escaped to the wild northern provinces [of Italy], and there have organized an army to overthrow Rome."

Phillips cautioned Brown against leading his volunteers into "some desperate enterprise, where they would be imprisoned and disgraced." Brown shrugged his shoulders. "I thought I could get you to understand this, . . ." he said. Deeply offended, William Phillips made for the door. "Captain," he said, "if you thought I was so stupid, why did you send for me?"

John Brown followed the younger man and laid his hand upon the journalist's shoulder. "When I turned to him," Phillips wrote,

> he took both my hands in his. I could see that tears stood on his hard, bronzed cheeks. "No," he said, "we must not part thus. I wanted to see you and tell you how it appeared to me. With the help of God I will do what I believe to be best." He held my hands firmly in his stern, hard hands, leaned forwards, and kissed me on the cheek, and I never saw him again.

Throughout October and November John Brown and his companions dawdled away their time at Osawatomie or on the border. During these weeks Brown was waiting for a sign from God, praying that he might be given an opportunity for action that would show the people back east that he was well occupied in Kansas.

The sign that he had waited for with such patience arrived on December 19, 1858, with the winter winds, in the person of Jim Daniels. "As I was scouting down the line," one of Brown's volunteers remembered, "I ran across a colored man." It was Jim Daniels, a fugitive slave from Missouri, selling brooms while looking for somebody to help him. He, his wife, children, and friends were part of an estate that was to be sold in the immediate future. Daniels wanted help to bring his family and friends out of Missouri before it was too late, and husband, wife, and children were split up by sale and separated forever.

John Brown wasted no time. The following night two rescue parties crossed over the line into Missouri and raided two plantations close by each other. John Brown himself liberated Daniels, his wife and four children, along with five other slaves. Also seized were horses, food supplies, and clothing for the use of the fugitives on the long winter trip to Canada.

After crossing back into Kansas, Brown sent the fugitives on ahead in a covered wagon while he and his volunteers stayed behind to harass and slow down the pursuers. When the slaves arrived a few days later at Osawatomie, they were hidden in an abandoned cabin on the open prairie. Neighbors brought food, gave them guns, told them to fight if attacked, but never to surrender. Armed men were set to watch the roads by day and night.

Search parties came after the slaves, and combed the timber along the Osage River and Pottawatomie Creek. Tired of a fruitless search, they left. John Brown headed the party northwards up the wagon trail to Lawrence, reaching the town on January 24, 1859 in freezing weather. Brown and his men were now criminals in the eyes of the federal government; they had deliberately violated the Fugitive Slave Act of 1850.

Northwards they went to the Nebraska line. They forded the Missouri at Nebraska City, passed over into Iowa, and headed east, clear across the state—through Tabor, Grinnell, Dalmanutha, Aurora, Des Moines, Iowa City, and Springdale. At the railroad depot close by Springdale they put the slaves in a box car on a train bound for Chicago, and from there to Detroit, where they were put upon the ferry that carried them across Lake St. Clair to safety in Canada. (See map below.)

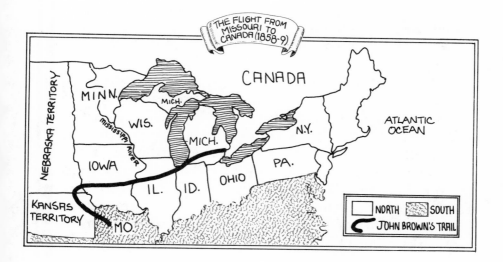

The flight from the Missouri border took a full three months and covered a distance of eleven hundred miles in the dead of winter. The journey through Kansas, Iowa, Illinois, and Michigan was a triumphal procession as men and women rallied to help the fugitives; to provide food, shelter, and clothing; and to scatter the sheriff's posses that came in pursuit, or tried to block the path. Through this aid to the fugitives, people expressed their open defiance of the Fugitive Slave Act, and their contempt for it. They were showing, too, their determination that in a free country the government should no longer be a tool for protecting the interests of the slaveholders and enforcing their demands.

John Brown showed skill and determination in leading the operation and bringing it to a successful close. Now, at last, the time for which he had waited so long had come. By the end of April he was back home at North Elba. Soon he would be on his way to Virginia and Harper's Ferry.

★   ★   ★   ★   ★

By 1859 John Brown had made a second big change in his original plan for the liberation of the slaves. He would not only found a free state in the South; he would launch the invasion from the federal armory of Harper's Ferry. As yet he had told nobody, not even his own followers, about this extraordinary decision. What could have been the reasons lying behind it?

Many people have assumed that because John Brown attacked Harper's Ferry, where rifles were made and stored in large quantities, he was after weapons. The fact is that John Brown took with him to Virginia enough weapons to supply a small army: two hundred Sharpe's rifles, dozens of revolvers, one thousand Collinsville pikes. He had no need of more. No, John Brown did not go to Harper's Ferry to get weapons; he made this perfectly clear to a newspaperman who spoke to him a few hours after the raid was over. Brown's remarks were published in the *Boston Journal* for Friday,

October 21, 1859, for all the world to read. *It was no part of his purpose*, the *Journal* writer reported, *to seize the public arms. He had arms and ammunition enough, furnished by the Massachusetts Emigrant Aid Society.*

Common sense confirms what Brown said. Suppose that Brown had wished to carry only a moderate number of rifles away from Harper's Ferry—say two thousand. In order to transport even so small a number, along with ammunition, he would have needed a train of twenty wagons and forty horses. Such a baggage train, if he had been foolish enough to think of such a thing, would have been a millstone around his neck. Moving southward at a snail's pace, it would have become bogged down amid trackless forests and steep mountain trails. When pursuers overtook the train, Brown would have been confronted with the choice of fighting for useless baggage or fleeing.

Brown, too, was reasonably well informed with respect to the location of other state arsenals throughout the South. As his armed forces grew, and needed more weapons, there were enough of these that he might raid, within striking distance of the hills.

The reason that Brown chose Harper's Ferry as his starting point was simple enough. The slaves of the South had no information about Brown's plan before he put it into operation. How, then, were black people to learn what was going on? His intention was to announce the beginning of the liberation movement with a trumpet blast—a blast, one might say, that would be heard around the world. The news would spread soon enough among the black people.

This is precisely what John Brown told Frederick Douglass just two months before the raid was launched, when the two men met at Chambersburg, Pennsylvania. "He thought," Douglass reported, "that the capture of Harper's Ferry would serve as notice to the slaves that their friends had come, and as a trumpet to rally them to his standard."

Why was Brown so rash as to believe that the slaves would flock to his standard as soon as they heard his trumpet? The answer lies both in his religious faith and the power of his imagination. Believing that a gigantic struggle with the tyranny of slavery loomed, he heard the tramping feet of millions who would now rise to assert the birthright of freedom, and to fight for its defense. It was music to his ears. All that was now needed was to sound the attack. This was the deed that would bring about the judgment and the will of God through the rising of the slaves.

If Brown's main reason for going to Harper's Ferry was to announce a liberation movement, why, then, did he occupy the arsenals and Hall's Rifle Factory, as well as the armory?

Occupying these facilities with two or three men each made no sense at all, no matter what Brown's objectives at Harper's Ferry were. Two men in a factory or an arms storage facility were incapable of offering effective resistance against determined attackers. The most that they could do, perhaps, was to fire the buildings in the event of retreat. These "occupations" further fragmented a tiny force that had already been split up to a ridiculous degree.

In June Brown bade farewell to his family. In July he found and rented a small farm on the Maryland side of the Potomac, some five miles from Harper's Ferry. Here he quietly assembled his arms and supplies, bringing them in a covered wagon from Chambersburg some forty miles to the north. His volunteers drifted in during the summer and fall, twenty-one of them in all. Some were men he had met or fought with in Kansas; some were black men; some were members of his own family or North Elba neighbors; a few came from Iowa and Canada. Last of the recruits to arrive was Francis Jackson Merriam, whom Franklin Sanborn had sent on from Boston. Merriam, a grandson of Francis Jackson, a wealthy Boston abolitionist, was wealthy in his own right. He joined the raiders early in October, bringing with him the welcome contribution of six hundred dollars in gold. "You can have my money and me with it," said the frail, handicapped youth.

To help with the housekeeping and to quiet neighbor suspicions that the "family" at the farm was not a normal one, Brown sent for his daughter Anne and his daughter-in-law Martha Evelyn. Martha Evelyn had married Oliver Brown the previous year; she was seventeen and Oliver was twenty. The young people, deeply in love, had a baby daughter who, that July, was barely five months old. Martha Evelyn and Annie could not cook in the basement kitchen, for it was crammed with supplies that included boxes of rifles and pikes. They had to make do with a wood stove in the living room upstairs.

Although twenty men had to live in close quarters, crammed like sardines into the tiny house, Brown, Annie, and Martha Evelyn created the picture of a nice, happy family. Jennie Chambers, a child who lived at the time on Bolivar Heights, just to the west of Harper's Ferry, recalled that Brown—who went by the name of Smith—"lived out at the Kennedy farmhouse on the Antietam Road with his two daughters. They were quiet unpretentious people, who had little to say to their neighbors, and that only for their good." Mr. Hoffmaster, who was "Mr. Smith's" next-door neighbor, also had good things to say about "Mr. Smith." "Smith," he said, "no matter where he came from, was a good neighbor, and a good preacher, too. He preached in the little church by the roadside."

As the time to launch the raid approached, Brown revealed the plan to his men: They were to attack Harper's Ferry. To some of them the news came as a great shock. They had joined Brown under the impression that they were going to Virginia in order to establish a base for running off slaves, not to attack a federal arsenal. There were heated discussions, but in the end Brown succeeded in quieting the dissenters. The men agreed to follow him "until he proved incompetent." It is unlikely that Brown ever overcame his own sons' inner doubts. Watson certainly, and maybe Oliver and Owen too, followed their father to the Ferry, not from a belief in victory but out of loyalty. The did not want to abandon the old man and leave him to die alone.

At the end of September Martha Evelyn and Annie left the farm and went back home to North Elba. Several weeks earlier John Brown had had his last meeting with Frederick Douglass at Chambersburg. Brown had gone to town on one of his many trips to pick up weapons and supplies. He wanted both to inform Douglass about the decision to attack Harper's Ferry and to invite him to join the army.

The two men met in an old stone quarry. Shields Green came with Douglass, John Henry Kagi with Brown. "John Smith" was disguised as a fisherman. "He looked every way like a man of the neighborhood," wrote Douglass, "and as much at home as any of the farmers around there. His hat was old and storm-beaten, and his clothing was about the color of the stone quarry itself."

Brown informed Douglass that he intended to attack Harper's Ferry, and asked him what he thought of the idea. Douglass at once opposed it "with all the arguments I could command." He pointed out that an attack upon Harper's Ferry would arouse the hostility of the entire country. Harper's Ferry, a spit of land with rivers on two sides, was a death trap; once Brown was in, the military would snap it shut, none of the invaders would get out alive. When Brown said that he would dictate terms of escape, because he would have hostages, Douglass gazed at him in amazement. Sheer illusion! he told Brown: "Virginia will blow you and your hostages sky-high, rather than that you should hold Harper's Ferry an hour."

The discussion continued all of the first day—a Saturday— and part of Sunday. Douglass was still committed to the old plan "of gradually and unaccountably drawing off the slaves to the mountains, as first proposed by Brown." Brown championed the new policy of "striking a blow which should instantly rouse the country."

Finally Douglass' patience was exhausted. He turned to Shields Green. You see how it is, he told his friend; there is an old plan, and a new plan. "I shall return home," said Douglass; "if you wish, you may go with me." Shields Green was silent. John Brown put his arms around his friend. "Come with me, Douglass," he pleaded, "when I strike, the bees will begin to swarm, and I shall want you to help hive them." Douglass, deeply moved by what he called "the dear old man's eloquence." turned away.

"What have you decided to do?" he asked Shields Green. "I believe I'll go wid de ole man," Green replied.

On Sunday morning, eight weeks later to the day, John Brown preached his last sermon at the little roadside church near the Kennedy farm. That evening, at eight o'clock, the raiders moved out. Three men, headed by Owen Brown, were left behind, to bring the supplies and the weapons and ammunition down to a schoolhouse by the Potomac, when they were sent for. John Brown and eighteen men headed down the trail. They went out into the darkness shrouded in long woolen shawls, single file through the shadows of the night.

12

YOUTH IS THE POLLEN
Burying the Dead, 1859-99

> For youth is the pollen
> That drifts through the sky
> And does not ask why.
>   —Stephen Vincent Benet,
>   "John Brown's Body."

John Brown lay on the floor of an office near the engine-house in Harper's Ferry, wounded and in the hands of his enemies. A faint tumult of voices penetrated the dimly lit room from outside. John Brown, at the center of the storm, lay quiet.

"Robber!" an angry bystander shouted.

"You," Brown answered calmly, "are the robbers."

"Blacks," he explained as reporters scribbled his words, "are as good as you and as precious in the sight of God."

Governor Wise, a highly educated and articulate man, stepped in to take the wind out of the old man's sails. "Mr. Brown," he said, "the silver of your hair is reddened by the blood of crime, and it is meet that you should [avoid] these hard allusions and think upon eternity."

Brown turned to him, Wise remembered, "a broken winged hawk with a fearless eye, and his talons set for further fight."

"Governor," he said,

I have from all appearances, not more than fifteen or twenty years the start of you in the journey to that eternity of which you kindly warn me; and whether my tenure here shall be fifteen months, or fifteen days or fifteen hours, I am equally prepared to go. There is an eternity behind and an eternity before, and the little speck in the center, however long, is but comparatively a minute. The difference between your tenure and mine is trifling and I want therefore to tell you to be prepared; I am prepared. You all have a heavy responsibility and it behooves you to prepare more than it does me.

John Brown was far more menacing to the South as an outspoken prisoner than as an invader. Again and again, he hammered home the message that slavery was a crime against God. "They could kill him," Douglass wrote, "but they could not answer him."

The governor spent that night at the Wager Hotel. The following day he put his five prisoners on the train and took them under heavy guard to Charles Town. Along with John Brown, Edwin Coppoc, and Shields Green, taken in the enginehouse, went John Copeland and Aaron Stevens, who had been captured on the first day of battle, Monday October 17. They were all lodged in the jail across the road from the Jefferson County courthouse.

Wise now pressed the trial forward with all possible speed. He was terrified by the thought of abolitionists streaming to the Virginia border to arm the slaves and to unleash the horrors of rebellion. Some antislavery people in Boston immediately began to plot Brown's rescue, just as Wise feared they would. Brown, said the governor, must be put out of harm's way before he could escape triumphantly to the North, where he might prepare fresh and even more dangerous attacks upon the South.

The trial proceedings began in Charles Town courthouse on Tuesday, October 25. Crowds thronged the town square outside the stately building; the courtroom itself was packed with people—lawyers, jurors, witnesses, townspeople and reporters. All over the country discussion of the attack on Harper's Ferry had reached fever pitch. People were thinking

"A Broken-winged hawk with a fearless eye."

John Brown of Osawatomie, wounded and a prisoner in the office at the firehouse, Harper's Ferry, October 18, 1859. This is how John Brown must have appeared to Governor Wise of Virginia when the two had their encounter shortly after the raid was over.
—Harper's Weekly Magazine, *1859*

and talking about little else. Everywhere meetings were being held to denounce Brown or to praise him. On October 25 Charles Town courthouse, with stately Grecian pillars decorating its entryway, became the focus of attention as the American nation watched, and listened.

A single week had passed since the end of the raid. This haste handicapped Brown severely in the preparation of his defense. Not only did he lack the time to secure an experienced lawyer, and the time for this lawyer to become familiar with the Virginia law and the facts of the case, he had little time to recover from his wounds and prepare to play a part in his own defense. The prosecution, therefore, had the advantage. It was in the hands of Andrew Hunter, a vigorous and able lawyer, who agreed entirely with Governor Wise that Brown should be disposed of "at double quick time."

"If you seek my blood," Brown burst out as the proceedings began, "you can have it at any moment without the mockery of a trial . . . you might spare yourselves that trouble. I am ready for my fate." But soon it dawned upon him that in the week since his arrest everything had changed. The eyes of the world were upon him; he had become, in a flash, the symbol of a cause. He was no longer an obscure member of a despised and hated antislavery minority defending itself as best it could from violence and persecution both in the North and the South. He stood for a new time, and a new movement.

John Brown was the symbol of that movement, and the Charles Town court was the place where he would deliver his message. This was the first stage of a new struggle in which he himself was going to die. He would offer up his life not only to free the slaves but also to free America from slavery. "Surely," as he wrote to Mary, "I can recover all the lost capital occasioned by that disaster [Harper's Ferry] by only hanging a few moments by the neck; and I feel quite determined to make the utmost possible out of a defeat."

On Wednesday, October 26, the Grand Jury met and handed down the indictment, or formal accusation, against John Brown and his companions. They were accused of treason, conspiring with slaves to rebel, and murder. They were, said the indictment, "evil persons not having the fear of God before their eyes, but moved by . . . the instigations of the devil."

Brown's plan was almost ruined when the trial opened the following day before Judge Richard Parker, a stern, dignified-looking jurist in the prime of life. Brown himself lay upon a cot, with a blanket to cover him. His head and face were so badly slashed by the sabre cuts he had received as to be almost unrecognizable. After Andrew Hunter had presented Virginia's case against Brown, Lawson Botts rose to his feet. Botts was one of the lawyers whom Judge Parker had asked to help with the defense; he read a telegram that he had just received from members of the Brown family in Ohio. There was a lot of insanity in the family, said these relatives, and John Brown, too, was mad. His life ought for this reason to be spared.

Promptly Brown raised himself up on his cot. "I reject," he said indignantly, "any attempt to interfere in my behalf on that score." His well-meaning relatives' telegram must have caused him much alarm. If the court accepted an insanity plea, he would be sent to the madhouse, his case discredited.

Judge Parker ruled that there was no insanity plea before the court, and the trial went on. But the danger was not over. Several weeks later, after Brown had been found guilty and sentenced to hang, fresh appeals were sent to Governor Wise urging him to pardon Brown because he was mad. Wise rejected these appeals. He may have been afraid that if he were to spare Brown's life there would be an angry outcry throughout the South, many of whose people were waiting impatiently for this rebel to suffer the death they felt he so well deserved. Beyond that, Governor Wise was an honest man: he had himself talked with Brown and had formed his own opinion about the state of Brown's mind. He knew perfectly well that John Brown was a sane man.

A stream of witnesses came before the court and testified about the raid and the killing done by both sides. To the chagrin of Hunter, his own son, Harry, testified that he and others had dragged William Thompson from the hotel and that he was one of those who shot the defenseless man down. John Brown, hearing for the first time how his neighbor's son had died, cried out in the courtroom.

Brown's lawyers tried to overturn the treason charge, arguing that he could not be guilty of treason against Virginia because he was not a citizen of that state. They denied that the raiders had any plans to incite slaves to kill whites, and put Brown's hostages on the stand to testify that they had been treated well.

On October 31, the jury brought in its verdict: guilty on all counts. Two days later, Judge Parker handed down his sentence. Before doing so he spoke to the prisoner. "Do you have anything to say?" he asked. John Brown rose from his cot. "I deny everything but what I have all along admitted," he said, "the design on my part to free the slaves. . . . That was all I intended. I never did intend murder, or treason, or the destruction of property, or to excite or incite slaves to rebellion, or to make insurrection."

This statement, as the prisoner saw it, was literally true. The sole purpose to which he had devoted the last years of his life was the liberation of the black people. He viewed this, not as a crime, but as a moral commitment. Holding slaves, as he saw it, not the liberation of slaves, was treason to the American Revolution and the free republic which it had brought into being.

He had resorted to violence, Brown continued, in order to free the slaves, but it was unjust that he should suffer the penalty of death for this. "Had I interfered," he said, "in behalf of the rich, the powerful, the intelligent, the so-called great, or in behalf of any of their friends, either father, mother, brother, sister, wife or children, or any of that class, . . . it would have been all right; and every man in this Court would have deemed it an act worthy of reward rather than punishment."

Here John Brown was making his own final judgment upon the times in which he lived. The early republican years, during which Brown was born and grew up, were a time of violence and bloodshed in American life. Native American people, by the tens of thousands, were driven off their lands, reduced to poverty, and killed. Throughout the South, slaveholders and speculators had been the first to benefit from endless acts of violence. In the Mexican-American War of 1846 U.S. armies had invaded Mexico and ripped from her lands where whites might plant slaves, find new wealth, and grow rich. Powerful people, Brown was saying, do not oppose violence and bloodshed when its purpose is to advance selfish ends and private greed.

"I see a book kissed," he said, "which I take to be the Bible. [The New Testament teaches me] that all things whatsoever I

would that men should do to me, I should do even so to them.
It teaches me, further, to 'remember them that are in bonds, as
bound with them.' I endeavored to act up to that instruction."

The prisoner now came to the conclusion of his speech. "I
believe," he said,

> that to have interfered as I have done, as I have always freely
> admitted I have done, in behalf of His despised poor, was not
> wrong, but right. Now, if it is deemed necessary that I should
> forfeit my life for the furtherance of the ends of justice, and
> mingle my blood further with the blood of my children and
> with the blood of millions in this slave country whose rights
> are disregarded by wicked, cruel, and unjust enactments, I say,
> let it be done.

Such were the words which twenty-two years later wrung
from Frederick Douglass, in an address delivered at Harper's
Ferry, the anguished judgment: *"his zeal in the cause of my
race was far greater than mine—it was the burning sun to my taper
light. . . . I could live for the slave but he could die for him."*

There was a silence in the court. Judge Parker then
pronounced sentence of death, and fixed the date: Friday,
December 2, 1859. To the horror of Governor Wise and
slaveholders everywhere, John Brown had one full month to
live.

He spent the time visiting with the people who thronged to
see him, and writing many letters to family and friends. "A
calm peace," he told John Jr., "perhaps like that which your
own dear mother felt in view of her last change, seems to fill
my mind by day and by night." His message to Mary was a
simple one:

> There will be poverty, sorrow, and tribulation to the end of
> your earthly path, for that is the fate that man was born for.
> Give thanks to our Father in Heaven, for "He doeth all things
> well." Kiss our children and grandchildren for me. Both of us
> have been called upon to make a sacrifice in our beloved cause,
> the cause of God and humanity. It is not too much, I would
> have sacrificed more! Consider well, before you decide to
> come and see me; it will only cause both of us more sorrow. In

the misery that you will have to endure, think always of the crushed millions who have none to comfort them. Do not forget the grief of the poor that cry, and have no help.

To his sons and daughters he said: "try to build again your broken walls, and to make the most of every stone that is left. . . . It is the ground of the utmost comfort to my mind to know that so many of you as have had the opportunity have given full proof of your fidelity to the great family of man."

Speaking to his friends, Brown assured them that he felt no disgrace in meeting death upon the gallows. "You cannot have forgotten," he wrote to cousin Luther Humphrey, "how and where our grandfather fell in 1776, and that he, too, might have perished on the scaffold, had circumstances been very little different."

The day of the execution drew near. Mary Brown left Philadelphia, where she had been staying, and came with friends by train to Harper's Ferry. She arrived on November 30, at the very same time as Colonel Robert E. Lee, whom President Buchanan had sent there, along with more than two hundred and fifty soldiers. His instructions were to protect the little town against a possible Northern invasion.

The President was responding to an appeal from Governor Wise, who, as the day of execution approached, grew more and more nervous. A series of fires in barns and haystacks in the Charles Town area threw him into a panic. Had these fires been set by abolitionist bandits? he asked himself. At his order armed men on horseback patrolled Jefferson County day and night; and four hundred militiamen and cadets were called up to provide protection for Charles Town itself on the day of execution.

On December 1st Mary Brown came to Charles Town to visit her husband. Together for the last time, they ate supper with Captain Avis, the jailer, and his wife, then said goodbye. Mary returned to Harper's Ferry to wait.

Friday, December 2 was a lovely day with a clear blue sky and a light, warm breeze. In the early morning troops were on the move, lining the streets and taking their positions in a field near the town where a gallows had been built. At eleven o'clock a wagon bearing a coffin was drawn up to the jail. John Brown came out and, walking between armed men, mounted the wagon and sat down upon the coffin; Captain Avis was at his side. Surrounded by an escort of soldiers the wagon was drawn off toward the fields. John Brown lifted his eyes to the hills that lay in a long blue line to the west. "This is a beautiful country," he said to his companion as they moved slowly along, "I have never had the pleasure of seeing it before."

Soon the condemned man stood upon the gallows with a rope around his neck and a hood over his head. "I am ready," said John Brown to the executioner, "but do not keep me waiting longer than necessary."

The troops marched and countermarched, forming two concentric squares. One of the officers in that company was Professor Thomas J. Jackson, of the Virginia Military In-

The Execution of John Brown

The execution scene in a field near Charles Town, (West) Virginia, December 2, 1859. This drawing appeared in Frank Leslie's Weekly *one week later, on December 10.*

stitute at Lexington, along with his cadets. He would be known to the world a year or so later as "Stonewall." On that field, too, was a young actor, John Wilkes Booth. Like Thomas Jackson, Booth joined the Confederate army when the war broke out in 1861. Just four years later he would assassinate the president of the United States.

Just before leaving the jail John Brown had handed a sheet of paper to one of the guards, and on it these words: "I, John Brown, am now quite certain that the crimes of this guilty land will never be purged away, but with blood. I had as I now think vainly flattered myself that without very much bloodshed it might be done." He was right. An ocean of blood would be spilled before slavery came to an end.

★   ★   ★   ★   ★

Early Saturday morning, December 3, Mary and her friends boarded the train at Harper's Ferry and went with John Brown's body on the first lap of the long trip home. Traveling by train and by ferry they reached New York City in the evening. Next day, Sunday, people thronged a funeral home in the Bowery, where the body was laid out, to pay their respects.

Louisa Williamson, a funeral-home worker, was one of the visitors. "None of his pictures," she wrote her brother later, "do him justice. I have never seen a finer looking man of his age, after such a death too. His countenance was as serene as if asleep."

Dawn, Monday, December 5. The mourners with their burden embarked upon the train for the journey up the Hudson Valley; throughout the long day the cars moved slowly northward. Bells tolled. Welcoming parties, clothed in black, thronged the wayside stations. Late that night the party reached Rutland, Vermont; Mary went to bed at midnight. Tuesday morning, in the dark hours before dawn, she went on, northward to Vergennes, a tiny village close to the shores of Lake Champlain. She and her friends crossed the lake by boat from Button Bay, landed on the western side near Westport, then placed the coffin upon a wagon for the final leg of the trip into the mountains. That night John Brown's body lay in state at Elizabethtown, seven miles west of Westport; young men of the neighborhood provided a guard. As night was falling the next day, December 7, John Brown was drawn home to North Elba.

The Reverend Joshua Young, minister at the Unitarian Church in Burlington, Vermont, arrived early the next day, Thursday, December 8, in time to conduct the funeral service. The Reverend hadn't thought he'd make it. Reaching Vergennes from Burlington the day before, Wednesday, Young found a storm raging over the lake, so that he could not cross. Early in the evening the storm died down, and the ferryman sailed him over. John Brown was an old friend of this ferryman's. "John Brown has crossed this ferry with me a hundred times," he said.

Having crossed Lake Champlain, Joshua Young pressed on through the night, finding the track by the light of the moon. Steep cliffs, great mountains, and deep woods hemmed in the road. He rode on hour after hour, in the awful silence, and, at dawn, he reached North Elba.

The funeral took place at one o'clock that Thursday, with a large party of mourners, at least half of whom were black. Rain was falling in a drizzle. Clouds were sailing swiftly across the wintry sky. Around, the primeval forest bent to the western wind; in the distance stood the majestic mountains, capped with snow.

Joshua Young opened the service. The people sang "Blow Ye the Trumpet, Blow"; the black people sang loudest of all. Wendell Phillips, famous abolitionist from Boston, gave the funeral oration. "Men believe more firmly in virtue," he said of the dead man in the coffin before him, "now that such a man has lived." The mourners sang another hymn; the coffin was lifted outside the house. The procession moved to the grave, hacked out in the frozen earth, a little way away at the base of a great rock. Joshua Young gave the prayer for the dead. John Brown's body was lowered into the ground and earth was thrown upon his coffin.

A few days later Mary received a letter from Captain John Avis expressing his "heartfelt sorrow for your bereavement." Avis enclosed with his note an inscription that John Brown had drawn up early in the morning on the last day of his life; he left instructions that this was to be engraved upon the old family stone that had recently been hauled to North Elba from Canton. He had written:

Oliver Brown born   1839 was killed at Harpers ferry Nov 17th 1859

Watson Brown born   1835 was wounded at Harper's ferry Nov 17th and died Nov 19th 1859

[Mary can] supply blank dates to above

John Brown born May 9th 1800 was executed at Charles Town, Va, December 2d 1859.

*   *   *   *   *

Years later the bodies of the men who died at Harper's Ferry were recovered and brought back to North Elba for burial. Watson's was the first of these. His body, along with that of Jeremiah Anderson, had been handed over to the medical college at Winchester—about twenty-two miles southwest of Harper's Ferry—for use in the dissecting room. After the Civil War it was discovered, identified, and returned to the family. At the burial service for Watson held at North Elba in 1882 Joshua Young officiated once more. John Brown Jr., now sixty years of age, read a letter that he had received from C.W. Tayleure, a South Carolina journalist who was at Harper's Ferry at the time of the raid, and who later became a soldier in the Confederate army.

Just after Lee's marines had ended their assault upon the enginehouse, Tayleure saw Watson lying upon the ground outside. "I gave him a cup of water to quench his thirst,"

Tayleure wrote. "He was very calm in tone and in look, very gentle. The look with which he searched my heart I can never forget."

"What brought you to Harper's Ferry?" Tayleure asked him.

"Duty, sir," Watson answered.

Tayleure snorted. "A strange idea of duty," he said, "sneaking in here at dead of night to murder innocent folks in their homes!"

Watson cut the journalist off short. "I am dying," he said, "I cannot discuss the question; I did my duty as I saw it."

In the years that followed Tayleure thought much about the raid, and its meaning for the American people, both slave and free. He ended his letter by telling John Jr. his conclusions.

"The sincerity, calm courage, and devotion to duty," he wrote, "which your father and his followers there manifested, impressed me profoundly. I have now come to see that the war was ordained of God for the extermination of slavery, and that your father was an elected instrument for the commencement of this good work."

Toward the end of the century the bodies of nine of the other members of John Brown's party who were killed during

The John Brown Gravesite, North Elba, New York
—from a photograph, date unknown

the raid were brought back to North Elba. Gathered up from the streets, the rivers, and the armory itself, the question had arisen, what was to be done with these remains? James Mansfield, a Harper's Ferry resident, was paid five dollars to get rid of them. Mansfield threw the bodies together into two wooden boxes and buried them in a mass unmarked grave at the edge of the Shenandoah River. They were discovered and dug up in 1899, and reburied at the John Brown farm next to John Brown and Watson. The bodies were still shrouded in the blanket shawls that the men had worn when they left the Kennedy farm on October 16, 1859. Once more the Reverend Joshua Young, now an old, white-haired man of seventy-six, conducted a funeral service. It was a sunny day, late in August. A detachment of soldiers from the 26th U.S. Infantry Division fired a volley over the dead.

EPILOGUE
MAKE WAY FOR LIBERTY

> Arnold Winkelried, Swiss patriot celebrated in legend, fell upon the enemy and gathered their spears to his own body, so that fellow fighters might break through the line. "Make way for Liberty!" he cried.

In December 1859 a winter of sorrow settled upon North Elba. Mary Brown had lost a husband and two sons; the Thompson family had lost two of its boys, William and Dauphin. Isabella and Martha Evelyn Brown were widows. Ruth Brown had lost the father whom she adored, and so too had her half-sisters Annie, Sarah and Ellen. "When the first terrible news came," Ruth wrote to the family friend, Mrs. Stearns, "I could not weep, nor sleep, and felt as though death would be a relief. To witness poor Mary's suffering was dreadful, but my tears seemed frozen, my heart was ready to burst, and all was dark."

Martha Evelyn, Oliver's beloved eighteen-year-old wife, gave birth to her child in the first week of January. Two nights later, while a snowstorm moaned about the little house and the fine snow drifted through the window frames, the baby died; Martha Evelyn followed it to the grave soon after. Stoically Mary recorded the loss. "The Lord gave, the Lord took away," she wrote. In another letter she thanked Mrs. Stearns for sending her a picture of Watson and Oliver: "I would praise God," she said, "that they ever lived and were counted worthy to suffer and die for so just a cause, and that He has left others for me to love and do for."

The Browns were now weary of North Elba with its long bleak winters and its sad associations. Salmon Brown was the first to leave and move west once more. California bound, he went with his wife, Abbie Hinckley, daughter of a North Elba farmer, their two daughters, and a few of his father's thoroughbred Saxon sheep.

Ruth and Henry Thompson followed Salmon at the end of 1863. Mary sold the John Brown farm to her son-in-law, Alexis Hinckley, and went as well. The Thompsons and their seven-year old child, with Mary and her three daughters, joined Salmon and Abbie in Iowa. In the spring of 1864 they all headed west on the long overland trip to the Pacific coast. Hauling the sheep in a wagon and driving their cattle ahead of them, they reached Red Bluff in Tehama County, at the northern end of the lovely Sacramento Valley, five months later. The cattle and sheep, it was said, were among the finest ever brought into Tehama.

Salmon Brown enjoyed a long life as a rancher and sheep raiser. After suffering losses in the blizzards of the early 1890's, he moved with his family to Portland, Oregon, and died there in 1918. His sisters, Annie and Ellen, married and raised ten children between them. Sarah remained single and devoted her life to caring for her mother. When Mary died at their home in San Jose in 1886, Sarah, who was an artist, gave time to teaching the children of Japanese immigrants. She found joy in the splendor of nature and the glories of the California sunset. A very private person, she kept the memories of her family, and its huge sacrifice, to herself. "Father's life went to the world," she told a reporter, "his daughter should be left alone."

Sarah's older half-brother, Owen, was one of the five who went to Harper's Ferry and returned alive. He, too, went to California, and settled far to the south of the others, at Altadena in the foothills of the San Gabriel Mountains. There Jason joined him in later years, with his wife Ellen; after her death the brothers lived together. When Owen died they buried him in a corner of his ranch. A huge rock forms his headstone, bearing the inscription

OWEN BROWN
Son of the Liberator
Died January 9, 1889, Aged 64 Years

John Brown's first son, John Brown, Jr., died six years after Owen. He was the only one of all John Brown's children to spend the remainder of his life in Ohio, the state where he was born. He and his wife, Wealthy, bought a farm on secluded South Bass Island, off the Ohio shore of Lake Erie.

Jason survived Owen and John Jr. by many years. He was, in some ways, his father's favorite son. "He is a very laborious, ingenious, temperate, honest, and truthful man," John Brown wrote to a Philadelphia friend from Charles Town jail, one week before his death, asking her help in locating Jason among people who would give him love and encouragement:

> he is very expert as a gardener, vine-dresser, and manager of fruit trees, but does not pride himself on account of his skill in anything; always has underrated himself; is bashful and retiring in his habits; is not (like his father) too much inclined to assume and dictate; . . . and is very poor. . . . He never quarrels, and yet I know that he is both morally and physically brave. He will not deny his principles to save his life, and "he turned not back in the day of battle." At the battle of Osawatomie he fought by my side. He is a most tender, loving, and steadfast friend.

When he was a very old man Jason's family brought him back to Ohio to die. Ever since childhood he had loved to watch the birds in their wheeling, soaring flight, and had dreamed of flying himself. He designed an airplane, and built a model of it. Shortly before World War I he foretold that "before ten years more you will hear of flights made across the Atlantic Ocean in flying machines. . . ."

★　　　★　　　★　　　★　　　★

An eminent lawyer has written that "there is nothing that people get used to so quickly, or endure so patiently, as injustice to others than themselves." This is true in today's world. It was certainly true in John Brown's time. Millions went about their business indifferent to the agonies of countless black Americans in chains, and to the wrongs that men, women, and children suffered day after day, generation after generation.

John Brown was not indifferent to these wrongs at any time from his childhood to his death, nor were the women whom he married, nor the children whom his wives and he raised. The evil of slavery, the suffering that it inflicted upon black people both in the North and the South, tormented his existence. From this compassion flowed a commitment to help the slaves win their freedom and to defend, if need be by force of arms, what they had won.

It was not easy then for people to grasp the nature and the depth of Brown's commitment. Frederick Douglass put it well in an address to black college students at Harper's Ferry in 1881. "Slavery," he told them, "had so benumbed the moral sense of the nation that . . . few could seem to comprehend that freedom to the slaves was John Brown's only object."

In the effort both to raise money to continue his antislavery work and to provide for his numerous family, John Brown encountered many failures—in land speculation, in the wool business, in his final disaster at Harper's Ferry. These massive failures did not break Brown's iron will to continue the struggle for his chosen goal. Brushing aside defeat and ignoring the imminence of death, he pressed on with his task until he could no longer breathe.

John Brown was a fighter against slavery, also a man of prophetic insight. He accepted the fact that lives would be lost in the struggle for the liberation of the black people. But in the war against slavery, which he felt was inevitable, he believed that bloodshed would be minimized if the slaves themselves were mobilized to fight in their own cause from the start.

Harper's Ferry was a first step, of inconceivable audacity, toward the implementation of Brown's vision. Yet Brown's own leadership there was weak and indecisive; this contrasts strangely with the bold and aggressive action which he took at Black Jack and Osawatomie. This indecisiveness led at once to disaster. Several factors may be suggested to account for this.

First of all, Brown greatly overestimated his own strength. Many slaves, he believed, would flock to his standard at once; he would march off to the mountains at the head of a large force at least several hundred strong. This, as the event proved, was fiction. Brown remained alone in the enemy's fortress, with his handful of prisoners and his tiny band of raiders, puzzled and confused.

In the second place, John Brown was incapable of separating the problems of supply—guns, ammunition, food, clothing, and tents for life in the mountains—from the tactics of the raid itself. A wiser commander would have cached these supplies in the hills long before the raid began; then he and his men, moving into Harper's Ferry, would have been burdened with little more than the weapons, the ammunition, and the food that they needed for the raid.

As it was, Brown clogged the whole operation by linking it with supply. He stored guns, pikes, and quantities of camp equipment at the Kennedy farm, then marched off to Harper's Ferry in the confident belief that Owen Brown would bring up these supplies when he called for them. This was folly. A glance at the map [page 7] shows that the slow-moving supplies would have to cross the river bridges into and out of Harper's Ferry *before* they could be safely stored in the mountains to the south, where Brown was headed. All that Brown's enemies had to do to bring an end to his operation was to win control of these bridges before Brown had time to bring the supplies down from the Kennedy farm. This is exactly what happened. Brown dawdled in Harper's Ferry not only because the slaves whom he expected did not arrive, but because Owen and his men could not transport the critically important weapons and other supplies quickly enough.

John Brown, finally, seriously underestimated his enemies. He believed that the Harper's Ferry and Charles Town authorities would be paralyzed with fear, and that he would have all the time in the world, therefore, to make his own moves. This was fatal. Nothing is more striking, on October 17, than the speed with which the Harper's Ferry townspeople reacted to the invasion and spread news of it; nothing is more striking than the speed with which the militia assembled, counterattacked, seized the Potomac and Shenandoah bridges, and caught Brown and his men, just as Douglass had predicted, like rats in a trap.

For the tragedy that resulted, John Brown alone was responsible. Many of Brown's own men, along with Frederick Douglass himself, had vehemently opposed his plan when they learned of it after arriving at the Kennedy farm. But John Brown had made up his mind. He was incapable of listening to, much less acting upon, the advice of people wiser than himself. Charles Plummer Tidd, one of the five survivors of the raid, expressed his own harsh judgment in conversations with Annie Brown years later. "I sometimes feel," he told her, "as if the Old Man murdered the boys after all that was said against going to Harper's Ferry, and the opposition of the whole company. . . ." Annie's own estimate of her father's enterprise was not so blunt, but equally honest. "Father's great mistake," she wrote, "seems to me to be having too much confidence in his own military ability and too little confidence in, and respect for, the capabilities of the United States troops. . . . He thought the slaves would flock to him, and that the masters would be paralyzed with fear and that they would make no resistance."

★   ★   ★   ★   ★

When the news of the Harper's Ferry raid hit the country, Abraham Lincoln was at his home in Springfield, Illinois, preparing a speech about Republican party policy on slavery. He delivered his address before an assembly of notables in New York City, February 1860. It was an important occasion. If Republicans liked what Lincoln said, and the way he said it, there was a good chance that they would select him as their presidential candidate in the November 1860 elections.

In this speech Lincoln went out of his way to assure Southerners that the Republicans had no desire, no right, and no power, if elected to office in Washington, to interfere with slavery where it existed in the States. All Republicans asked, said he, was that slavery should not be allowed to advance one single inch further into American territories. To underline the fact that Republicans had no hostility toward Southerners, or Southern slavery, Lincoln introduced into his address a special reference to John Brown. Republicans would never, like John Brown, said he, seek to abolish slavery by force and to wipe it out of existence with fire and sword. John Brown's effort, said Lincoln,

> was peculiar. It was not a slave insurrection. It was an attempt by white men to get up a revolt among slaves, in which the slaves refused to participate. . . . That affair, in its philosophy, corresponds with the many attempts, related in history, at the assassination of kings and emperors. An enthusiast broods over the oppression of a people till he fancies himself commissioned by Heaven to liberate them. He ventures the attempt, which ends in little else than his own execution.

Lincoln was certainly right in presenting Brown as an "enthusiast"—a person committed to a cause with single-minded will. But he paid no attention to the heart of Brown's message—that in the coming struggle against slavery black people themselves must be mobilized, and that these people were in a position to play a decisive role. The Republicans, indeed, nominated Lincoln as their candidate; he and they won the November elections. Both in the presidency and in Congress an antislavery party came to power in 1861, committed to blocking any further territorial expansion of slavery. Now, just as John Brown had predicted when he talked with William Phillips in 1858, the Southern states trooped out of the Union, and set up their own independent Confederacy; four years of violent, heartbreaking war began.

Very soon the harsh necessities of war obliged Lincoln to understand that what John Brown had tried to do was not so "peculiar" after all. By the fall of 1862 General Robert E. Lee was racing northward across Maryland; Lincoln saw the Union at the very edge of destruction. He concluded that the Union could not be saved, nor the Confederacy overthrown, without abolishing slavery and without summoning the black people themselves to fight under the American flag. With his Emancipation Proclamation of January 1863, Lincoln emblazoned the word *Freedom!* upon the Union banners; he resorted to fire and sword in order to accomplish a great social change. Nearly 200,000 black soldiers marched off to war with guns in their hands; 37,000 of them died.

In April 1865 Abraham Lincoln paid for his decision with his life. John Wilkes Booth—who, it will be remembered, was with the military guard at Brown's execution—struck him down at Ford's Theater in Washington, D.C. In killing Lincoln, as he himself said, he was only killing yet one more traitor.

Northern soldiers did not think that Lincoln was a traitor any more than they thought that Brown was. Dozens of verses to a song called *John Brown's Body* were composed, and spread through the Army. Once verse said

> His sacrifice we share! Our sword will victory crown! . . .
> For freedom and the right remember old John Brown!
> His soul is marching on.

Black soldiers put their own special verses to the John Brown tune. Speaking of the South, of the country itself, they sang

> They will have to bow their foreheads to their colored kith and kin,
> They will have to give us house-room or the roof will tumble in!
> As we go marching on.

In the long run, what mattered more than the failure at Harper's Ferry was the raid's impact upon the American people. John Brown and his tiny twenty-one man army awakened millions to the reality of the coming war. Tens of thousands took up the cause and followed in their footsteps.

The summons that John Brown uttered at Harper's Ferry, that obliged the world to wake up, and listen, is his title to immortality: *Make Way for Liberty.*

APPENDIX

JOHN, DIANTHE AND MARY BROWN, AND THEIR CHILDREN

Owen Brown = Ruth Mills

JOHN BROWN
= Dianthe Lusk (1)   = Mary Day (2)

John Jr.	1821		Sarah	1834–43
Jason	1823		Watson	1835–59
Owen	1824		Salmon	1836–1918
Frederick	1827–1831		Charles	1837–43
Ruth	1829		Oliver	1839–59
Frederick	1830		Peter	1840–43
unnamed son b. & d. 1832			Austin	1842–43
			Annie	1843
			Amelia	1845–46
			Sarah	1846
			Ellen	1848–49
			unnamed son	1852
			Ellen	1854

Birth and also death dates are given for those who died in childhood, or at Harper's Ferry in 1859.

THE HARPER'S FERRY RAIDERS

Killed October 17-19th 1859

Anderson, Jeremiah
Brown, Oliver
Brown, Watson
Kagi, John Henry
Leary, Lewis
Leeman, William H.
Newby, Dangerfield
Thompson, Dauphin
Thompson, William
Taylor, Stewart

Executed by the State of Virginia

Brown, John .... December 2, 1859

Copeland, John A. .... December 16, 1859
Coppoc, Edwin .... December 16, 1859
Cook, John E.★ .... December 16, 1859
Green, Shields .... December 16, 1859

Hazlett, Albert★ .... March 16, 1860
Stevens, Aaron D. .... March 16, 1860

★ Escaped, and later captured

Survivors

Anderson, Osborn P.
Brown, Owen
Merriam, Francis Jackson
Tidd, Charles Plummer
Coppoc, Barclay

BIBLIOGRAPHY

PRIMARY SOURCES

The Boyd B. Stutler Collection is the greatest assemblage of unpublished source material relating to John Brown. It is housed at the Archives and History Center of the West Virginia Department of Culture and History: Capitol Complex, Charles Town, West Virginia. The collection includes an indispensable periodical guide by Boyd B. Stutler, "John Brown in Periodical Literature, 1845-1959." Typescript, Charles Town, W. Virginia, 1959, with card additions to 1961.

Much of the Stutler Collection has been placed upon microfilm, available on interlibrary loan from the Ohio Historical Society: 1985 Velma Avenue, Columbus, Ohio, 43211. The eight reels contain Brown family letters, Perkins and Brown letterbooks, accounts of the Kansas struggle, including the invaluable notes of Kansas historian William E. Connelly, scrapbooks with press clippings, and memoirs, bibliographies and manuscript inventories.

The Ohio Historical Society also possesses its own archive, the Correspondence of John Brown, Jr., which contains the largest single surviving group of John Brown's own letters.

This material, too, is available from the Ohio Historical Society on interlibrary loan, in microfilm form.

Archival material indispensable for the study of Kansas in the John Brown years is contained in Record Group 59 of the General Records of the Department of State in the National Archives and, in particular, State Department Territorial Papers: Kansas, 1854-61. These papers are available on microfilm (Microcopy No. 218, two reels) from the National Archives and Records Service: General Services Administration, Washington, D.C.

John Brown materials are scattered throughout a number of other depositories. For a useful listing see Richard O. Boyer, *The Legend of John Brown: A Biography and a History* (New York: Alfred A. Knopf, 1973), 613-622. Some of this material is also available on microfilm. Richard Boyer spent many years bringing together transcripts of these sources for his own files. The Richard Owen Boyer Papers consist of 57 boxes presently in the collection of the Massachusetts Historical Society. These papers constitute a major resource for the study of John Brown.

Students at present are handicapped by the absence of systematically organized published records relating to John Brown, his family, and his associates. *A John Brown Reader* is a pioneering collection of materials under the editorship of Louis Ruchames (New York: Abelard-Schuman, 1959) that has not yet been surpassed. A revised, slightly abridged edition was published by Grosset and Dunlap in 1969 under the title of *John Brown: The Making of a Revolutionary* (paperback). A number of documents fundamental for an understanding of Brown may be found in one or the other of four early biographical studies: Richard J. Hinton, *John Brown and his Men* (New York: Funk and Wagnall, 1894); Franklin B. Sanborn, *The Life and Letters of John Brown* (Boston, 1891; reissued New York: Negro University Press, 1969); Oswald Garrison Villard, *John Brown, 1800-1859: A Biography Fifty Years After* (Boston, 1910; reissued New York: Alfred A. Knopf, 1943); and James C. Malin, *John Brown and the Legend of Fifty-Six* (Philadelphia: American Philosophical Society,

1942). Sanborn's material is poorly organized and not easy to use; Villard not infrequently deletes portions of the documents reproduced without notifying the reader.

BIOGRAPHY

The exploration of John Brown as biographical subject is still at the beginning. That is not to say that there are no biographies of Brown; on the contrary, there are many; but, too often, they are highly partisan. On the one side John Brown has been portrayed as a Puritan hero, a plaster saint, or both. On the other side he appears as horse-thief or terrorist, with a dose of madness and fanaticism thrown in. C. Vann Woodward's essay "John Brown's Private War," in *The Burden of Southern History* (Baton Rouge: Louisiana State University Press, 1960), ably and temperately states the anti-Brown position. James Redpath's *The Public Life of Captain John Brown* (Boston: Thayer and Eldridge, 1860), in the first biography to appear, depicts the saint-hero. It is fair to say that Redpath repudiated his biography after the Civil War, when he learned the truth about the Pottawatomie massacre. Of the four early biographies listed above, under Primary Sources, three—by Hinton, Sanborn, and Villard—follow, on the whole, the hero-worshipping tradition. Malin remains the leading exponent of the "horse-thief" theory. Another biography from this period is highly favorable to Brown yet in a class by itself for perceptiveness: W.E.B. DuBois, *John Brown* (Philadelphia, 1909; reissued as an International Publishers paperback, New York, 1974).

Three biographies of John Brown appeared during the 1970s: Stephen B. Oates, *To Purge This Land with Blood: A Biography of John Brown* (New York: Harper and Row, 1970;

reissued as a paperback, Amherst: University of
Massachusetts Press, 1984); Jules Abels, *Man on Fire: John
Brown and the Cause of Liberty* (New York: Oxford University
Press, 1971); and Richard O. Boyer, *The Legend of John Brown*,
cited above. Each of these books has excellencies that
differentiate it from all preceding biographical studies. Abels
achieves an approach that is both critical and objective, but he
has difficulty making his subject live. Oates has scrutinized
many original sources, but he devotes less than twenty
percent of his pages to the first fifty of the fifty-nine years of
John Brown's life. Boyer remedies this deficiency by pioneering a detailed exploration of Brown's early years. His volume
ends in October 1855, at the moment when Brown's life was
soaring to its tragic climax. Boyer, alas, did not live to complete his task. The second volume, for which Alfred A. Knopf
had waited so long, was never published.

HARPER'S FERRY

John Brown studies are deficient with respect to the history
of the 1859 raid itself. We lack a major, full-length study of the
thirty-six hours that elapsed between the time that John
Brown and his men left the Kennedy farm on the evening of
October 16 and Lee's storming of the enginehouse on the
morning of Tuesday, October 18. Merritt Roe Smith's
*Harper's Ferry Armory and the New Technology: The Challenge of
Change* (Ithaca: Cornell University Press, 1977) and Allan
Keller's *Thunder at Harper's Ferry* (Englewood Cliffs, N.J.:
Prentice-Hall Inc., 1958) are of help, though Keller's book is
handicapped by a total absence of maps to illustrate the loca-
tion and development of the armed struggle.

THE UNITED STATES 1800-1860

Useful information on the cultural context of John Brown's life during the early republic and in the mid–century crisis of American society is provided by the following:

R.C. Buley, *The Old Northwest: Pioneer Period, 1815-1840* (Bloomington: Indiana University Press, 1950. 2 vols.). The standard study of Ohio and the Northwest in the time of John Brown's youth.

Frederick Douglass, *Life and Times of Frederick Douglass* (1892; reissued as a paperback, New York: Collier Books 1962). Douglass's famous autobiography is a fundamental source for the study of John Brown.

T.H. Gladstone, *The Englishman in Kansas, or Squatter Life and Border Warfare* (1857; reissued by University of Nebraska Press, Lincoln, 1971). A classic and vividly written account of conditions in Kansas in 1855-56 by an English traveler.

Grace Boulder Izant, *Hudson's Heritage: A Chronicle of the Founding and the Flowering of the Village of Hudson* (Kent, Ohio: Kent State University Press, 1985). A lifelong resident's charming study of the frontier town in which John Brown grew to manhood.

Robert Leslie Jones, *History of Agriculture in Ohio to 1880* (Kent, Ohio: Kent State University Press, 1983). Graphic account of the transformation of Ohio agriculture in the period from 1780 to 1850, with, of course, a chapter on sheep and the wool industry.

Edgar J. McManus, *Black Bondage in the North* (Syracuse, N.Y.: Syracuse University Press, 1973). Provides information with respect to the origins, development, and decline of slavery in the North. This was an historical reality of primary importance in moulding John Brown's attitude to the struggle for black equality as part of the overall confrontation with slavery in America.

Milton Meltzer, *Bound for the Rio Grande: The Mexican Struggle, 1845-1850* (New York: Alfred A. Knopf, 1974). An unsurpassed account, by an eminent historian, of the mid-century struggle and the crisis that it generated.

Allan Nevins, *The Ordeal of the Union* (New York: Scribner's, 1947. 2 vols.). Indispensable for the unfolding of the national political crisis of the 1850s.

Benjamin Quarles, *Black Abolitionists*, and *Allies for Freedom: Blacks and John Brown* (New York: Oxford University Press, 1969 and 1974, respectively). Two books that are invaluable for their full information concerning black antislavery fighters and John Brown's relationships with them.

John Anthony Scott, *Hard Trials on my Way: Slavery and the Struggle Against It, 1800-1860* (New York: Alfred A. Knopf, 1974). Chronicles the simultaneous expansion of slavery and the antislavery movement during the span of John Brown's life.

Wilbur H. Siebert, *The Underground Railroad from Slavery to Freedom* (1898; reissued Gloucester, Mass.; Peter Smith, 1968). Classic study of the struggle by and on behalf of fugitive slaves, including John Brown's work.

George R. Taylor, *The Transportation Revolution 1815-1860* (New York: Holt, Rinehart and Winston, 1951). A comprehensive study of the Northern industrial revolution that conditioned the evolution of American society during the first half of the 19th century.

INDEX

181